CLEARING
the BASES

CLEARING the BASES

Juiced Players, Monster Salaries,
Sham Records, and a Hall of Famer's
Search for the Soul of Baseball

MIKE SCHMIDT WITH
GLEN WAGGONER

HarperCollins*Publishers*

HarperCollins books may be purchased for educational, business, or sales promotional use. For information, please write: Special Markets Department, HarperCollins Publishers, 10 East 53rd Street, New York, NY 10022.

Designed by Nancy Singer Olaguera

Printed on acid-free paper

Library of Congress Cataloging-in-Publication Data is available upon request.

ISBN-10: 0-06-085499-5
ISBN-13: 978-0-06-085499-7

06 07 08 09 10   RRD   10 9 8 7 6 5 4 3 2 1

My parents, Lois and Jack Schmidt of Dayton, Ohio, gave me every possible opportunity to cultivate and expand my life. Love, discipline, education, faith—they provided everything a young man could need from a family, including a wonderful sister, Sally.

My wife, Donna, has been my mentor, best friend, and one true love for thirty-two years—as well as mother to Jessica Rae and Jonathan, two bright and shining stars who continue to light up my life.

To all of them, I dedicate this book in appreciation of the unconditional love they have showered on me.

CONTENTS

INTRODUCTION Take Me Out to a Ball Game   1

1   A Simple Game   7

2   United, We Stood   21

3   The Best of Times   39

4   Turn Out the Lights   55

5   All Good Things   63

6   The Worst of Times   71

7   Looking for an Edge   81

8   Finding the Abyss   87

9   Better Than Ever   103

10   The Boom-Boom Years   121

11 Deck the Hall 139

12 What About Pete? 151

13 Summer School 165

14 Still the Best Game in Town 185

ACKNOWLEDGMENTS 197

INTRODUCTION
Take Me Out to a Ballgame

The strike of 1994, culminating in the cancellation of the 1994 World Series, seemed like the last straw for baseball fans. The decade-long bickering and sniping between owners and players had come to a head. To many, it seemed like a fight between the Rich and the Also Rich, Greed vs. More Greed. The fans, the people who shelled out a couple hundred bucks to take the kids out to the ballpark for a game, were the biggest losers.

Fans had simply had enough of what they saw as overpaid players wanting more money from whining owners. Although baseball came back in 1995, thanks to a judge in the Bronx who ruled that the owners were engaging in unfair labor practices, a lot of fans didn't. By 1996, attendance was down by 15 percent across baseball. The game appeared to have lost its historic hold on many Americans' lives.

I know it had on mine.

Except for my induction into the Hall of Fame in late summer of 1995, I had lost interest in baseball, and it in me. I was living in Florida, and my attention was primarily focused on family and golf. (I had aspirations of turning pro and playing on the Senior Tour when I turned fifty. I came close. But that's another story for another time.)

I only occasionally watched baseball on TV. From 1992 through 2000, the only game I attended—at least one that didn't involve a special public appearance—was Opening Day for the Marlins organization in 1993.

Then it happened: the 1998 season, Mark McGwire vs. Sammy Sosa, the home run race that captivated baseball fans everywhere.

I was hooked. In September, I followed every at-bat of both guys. I remember once being at an airport, watching their first at-bats on a TV in a bar, among a crowd that was ten deep. I waited until the last minute to board the flight, and then I asked the pilot if he could update us, not on the games, just on Mac and Sammy. The pilot would come on and say, "After two at-bats, neither Sammy nor Mark has homered." As soon as the plane landed, I ran to the nearest TV.

It was awesome. I knew these guys could hit—*everybody* knew that—but who knew they were such great showmen? I was watching at home on September 8, the night McGwire hit number 62. It was magical. I had goose bumps. Then, when he went into the stands and hugged Roger Maris's family, I cried along with the rest of America.

Can you believe it happened against the Cubs, with Sammy watching? When they showed Sammy clapping in right field, and then hugging Mark near the dugout, I fell in love with baseball all over again.

Only in baseball, a sport whose history is well known and cherished, a sport that moves slowly enough for all fans to appreciate the moment, a sport whose fans are so connected to the game's past, could a scenario like this pack such an emotional wallop.

So the Mac & Sammy Show brought me back to baseball, just

as it did millions of fans across the country. It was an escape from the daily bickering between owners and players, and an escape from the public focus on greedy, overpaid players. It offered fans across the country a headline, a prime topic for water cooler and lunch table conversation.

The 1998 season offered us all a reason to come back to baseball. Little did any of us realize at the time that our game's renaissance had an ugly side.

"If I had played in the 1990s, I would have used steroids. Why? Because I'm human."

I said those words on the HBO show *Costas Now* in July 2005. I said them in response to a direct question from Giants running back Tiki Barber. I said them in the heat of a panel discussion—Bob Costas and NBC's Jimmy Roberts were the other participants—on the state of sports in America today.

Much as I wish I'd thought more carefully before I spoke—it was uncharacteristic of me not to, I assure you—what I said wasn't far from the truth. Hey, when I played I was the typical power hitter looking for an edge to keep up with my competition. Why, in a different time and a different situation, wouldn't I have fallen victim to the use of steroids? Certainly I would have been tempted.

But *only* tempted, I am now certain. In my research for this book, I have thought long and hard about the use of performance-enhancing drugs in baseball. (You'd expect that, of course, given the thousands of headlines and millions of words devoted to the subject in the past few years.) I have come to understand how steroid use has spread to the high school and college level. I have reflected on the destructive impact steroids have had on baseball's precious history, its records, and the very integrity of the sport.

And I believe in my heart that I would have chosen *not* to use steroids.

But I also believe I understand what drove those who did.

The Steroid Era in baseball—roughly, 1990–2005—was fueled by a motive as old as the game itself: the search for a competitive edge.

But other factors have played major, if less threatening, roles in transforming baseball in the last three decades.

Free agency, more than anything else, created today's game. By righting a major wrong in the way baseball went about its business, the great Marvin Miller and the early pioneers (Curt Flood, Andy Messersmith, Dave McNally) brought baseball into synch with the American concept of a free market system.

But there's no such thing as a free lunch, and a downside to free agency is that loyalty to team is a forgotten concept in baseball today. Pedro Martinez is a Red Sox star who helps break the Curse of the Bambino, he almost becomes a Yankee, and suddenly he's a Met—all in the space of, what, three months? Admit it, that little dance made your head spin. And now, Johnny Damon's a *Yankee?*

Is it good for the game that the free agent declaration and signing periods are nearly as big news as the playoffs and the World Series? I don't think so.

And what about baseball's fundamental economic structure, one that has greatly widened the gap between rich and poor in recent decades? Is it good for baseball that one team has a payroll of more than $200 million, and can buy a Gary Sheffield one year and a Randy Johnson the next, while sixteen of their competitors have payrolls under $60 million? I don't think so.

Baseball's soul resides in its history. Can you imagine playing this coming season with the past being a void? I mean, if all that happened before Opening Day 2006 were to be washed from our memories, what would the new season be like?

Football and basketball, I submit, wouldn't be hurt all that much by the loss of their history. They are sports of Right Now. For baseball, the loss of its past would be unthinkable. Baseball is Now, seen through the prism of Then.

That's why every baseball fan knows what 30–100–.300 means, and can rattle off the names of a dozen or more players capable of putting up those numbers year after year. That's why winning 20 games is important. That's why fans go bonkers in Hall of Fame debates. That's why the Pete Rose saga tore at the game's heart.

Why? Because baseball history tells us these things matter.

If you're willing to accept that baseball needs its history, then you need to know about the elements that make today's game different from the game of thirty years ago. How else can you reasonably compare Bonds to Aaron, or Clemens to Koufax, or A-Rod to Schmidt? You need to know about major leaps in bat technology, smaller ballparks, smaller strike zones, hotter balls, much better conditioning, weaker pitching—and bigger, much bigger, payoffs for the long ball.

Drugs aside, these factors on their own have collectively had a huge, transformative effect on baseball's precious history.

That is, on baseball's soul.

America has changed dramatically in the last thirty years, both for good and for bad. And so has baseball.

That shouldn't come as a shock, yet somehow it does. Something keeps telling us that baseball must never change. We want to believe baseball is an immutable, permanent factor of our American culture, our heritage, our personality. The way we remember it being when we were growing up.

Sorry to break the news, but the very foundation of baseball's enduring greatness—its slow-moving pace, its exquisite subtlety, its deep bond with loyal fans—is being shaken by the nature of the times in which we live.

This book, based on my experiences playing baseball at the highest level and on my analysis of its evolution over the last three decades, conveys my love and understanding of the game, but also explores some fears I have about its future. It exposes much of me, and what I stood for. In fact, it exposes more than anything I ever did when I wore the number 20 on my back. My hope is that it serves the game.

Baseball will survive. It's too great a game not to. Its hold on America is too strong. There's still no clock to run out. You still have to get the last three outs to win. The game's still so perfect that, when a ground ball is fielded in the hole at short, a good throw gets the batter by a step. There's still nothing more thrilling than a triple, with the ball and the runner reaching third together in a cloud of dust. And you still can't beat a game-winning homer in the bottom of the ninth.

Baseball's not permanently broken, just a little banged up. If we can slow things down a little, if baseball can reconnect with its past, if we can go back to what really matters, then I believe baseball can once again become—and remain—America's Game.

1 A Simple Game

It was a bright yellow 1971 Corvette Sting Ray fastback, and the asking price was just under $10,000. That little beauty, the car I'd dreamed of my whole life growing up in Dayton, Ohio, would eat up nearly a third of the $32,500 signing bonus I got for being selected by the Phillies in the second round of the 1971 draft. But what was money for? To spend, baby! I had to have it.

As a young athlete I was pretty good in all sports, with baseball playing second fiddle to basketball. But because of two knee operations before I turned eighteen, my basketball dreams ended early, and no college had serious interest in me as a baseball player.

My senior year in high school, I took a liking to one course, drafting. Using a T-square and a triangle to create working drawings lit my fire, and the best architectural college around was Ohio University. Coincidentally, OU also had the best baseball program around. So off I went to become an architect and to try out for the freshman baseball team. Little did I know what lay ahead of me.

Only one major league scout, Tony Lucadello, of the Phillies, even knew I was alive. Tony had been following me since I was in Little League. Keep in mind, now, I wasn't a big prospect. I was never all-city or all-state. I wasn't even offered a college scholarship. Still, there were a couple of guys who kept me in their back pocket, and Tony was one of them. Tony saw me play from time to time, but always kept a low profile when he was there. Sometimes he'd watch from his car in the parking lot, or alone on a hill overlooking the field. He knew I was going up to Ohio University to study architecture and play ball, but he also knew that if anybody could develop me as a player, it was OU's Bob Wren, one of the best baseball coaches in college ball. First, of course, I had to make the freshman team.

I won't bore you with details of my college life, but those four years at Ohio University set the stage for all that has followed. College is where I became a man, and a serious baseball prospect.

Suffice it to say, my baseball life came together my sophomore year. Rich McKinney, Ohio's all-everything shortstop, signed a pro contract, and I was next in line at the position. Coach Wren gave me a shot at the job in the fall, knowing he'd always have other options come spring. The experiment worked. I was all-conference that year, and all-American the following two seasons. All of a sudden I was on a lot of scouts' lists. I went off to college as an utter unknown; I left as a projected first-round pick. Not too shabby for a walk-on.

Now, back in 1971, the major league baseball annual amateur draft wasn't any big deal, at least not to the general public. No TV coverage, very little in the newspapers. But it was plenty big around my house, I can tell you that. The Phillies had a lousy record in 1970, so they had the sixth pick in 1971, and they used it to take Roy Thomas, a right-handed pitcher. They took me with their first pick in the second round, number 30 overall.

Some pretty good ballplayers came out of that 1971 draft. Guys like Frank Tanana (13), Rick Rhoden (20), and Ron Guidry (65). Oh, yeah, and there was a California kid just out of high school who was taken by the Royals right before me at number 29—fellow by the name of George Brett.

Right there, in June 1971, came my first big break in baseball, not so much because of who took me but because of who didn't. You see, a local Orioles scout named Jack Baker had me at the top of his prospects list. Lucky for me, though, he couldn't persuade his bosses back in Baltimore to take me. I was a shortstop at the time I was drafted, but I'd soon be moved to third. Just imagine trying to break in behind Brooks Robinson, who was coming off his tenth straight All-Star season and had four more ahead of him!

The Phillies sent Tony Lucadello to my home in Dayton, Ohio, to get my name on a contract. I'll never forget him sitting in our living room with my father and me, saying "Mr. Paul Owens has instructed me to offer you $25,000 if you'll sign this contract." (*$25,000! To play baseball!*) But my father would have none of that. Actually, he told Tony to go home and come back with more money, much as Scott Boras says today with his top draft picks. (Sure.) Well, Tony came back the next morning, and we talked some more, and Dad sent him away again. We did a couple more go-rounds, and finally we agreed on $32,500 plus an incentive bonus that could add up to another $7,500—$2,500 for each minor league classification I jumped.

Thinking about it now, Dad did pretty well by me. Back then, it was either take what they offered or take a job dipping ice cream cones in my father's restaurant. But what really sealed the deal—besides that extra $7,500—was an invitation to come to Philadelphia for a weekend series against the Giants and work out with the big club.

Where do I sign?

• • •

Growing up in Dayton, Ohio, I played ball all the time, but never really believed I'd ever play in the big leagues. But, all of a sudden, the Phillies are going to pay me to put on a big league uniform, with those beautiful red Adidas shoes. It still gives me goose bumps, just thinking about it.

My baseball world up until that time had been very small. Just Dayton and Athens and Ohio University. Growing up, I was a Reds fan. Crosley Field, where my dad had taken me to ball games, was hallowed ground. There was center fielder Vada Pinson in his shiny shoes, one of the most underrated players of all time in my book. Wally Post. Johnny Temple. Those guys, they weren't really human in my mind. They were gods. I never thought there was any way I'd meet those guys or get close to them, let alone be one of them. But I knew all of them, every one of them, knew them by their names and by their stats. Bob Purkey, Jim O'Toole, Gene Freese: they were my guys, my team, and they were mostly the same guys, every year, all the time I was growing up. That's a huge difference between then and now. Back then, you knew the players on your team, and looked forward to tracking their careers, from one season to the next. You didn't have to learn a whole roster of new names every year.

After I signed with the Phillies, my father and I boarded a plane for Philadelphia for the biggest weekend of my life. We were picked up at the airport and taken directly to Veterans Stadium, which, at the time, was the newest and coolest stadium in baseball. When we arrived my heart was pounding. It was like nothing I'd ever seen. It looked like a giant flying saucer. It made Crosley Field, which had opened in 1912, look like a decrepit relic.

In high school, I played third, short, and occasionally pitched. But by college I was a shortstop full-time, and when I arrived in Philadelphia that weekend, whom do I see but *Chris Speier*, the starting shortstop for the San Francisco Giants. Chris was one of the first nineteen- to twenty-year-old kids to get to the big leagues.

Just *seeing* him play was a big deal. But to get to take infield practice on the *same field*? Life couldn't get any better.

My father and I entered the clubhouse to meet Phillies manager Frank Lucchesi before I suited up. It was so surreal, as if I were in a dream. I was shaking like a leaf. This wasn't like any locker room I had ever envisioned, much less seen. Crosley Field, the only other major league park I'd ever been to, had an old white house outside the stadium where the players dressed. To get to the field, the players had to walk on a little runway beneath the stadium. Well, at the Vet, the clubhouse was nearly fifty yards long. And the lockers were more like full-size rooms. Leather chairs. Red carpet. TV sets. And real, live big league baseball players. Could this get any better?

Ironically, the first player I met in that room was the player whose job I'd end up taking: John Vukovich. He'd just been called up to fill out the roster when somebody went on the DL, and he was scheduled to start that night. Vuk, who was the next in line for the third base job in Philadelphia, looked exactly like a big league ballplayer is supposed to look: muscular, handsome, trim, cut biceps. All he had on was this wide-band jock strap—the first one of those I'd ever seen—over his sliding pads, with "VUK" printed in big, black letters on the front.

(Vuk and I went on to become minor league teammates, major league teammates, opposing players, and most important, good friends.)

I walked around some more, met some more guys, and then Mr. Lucchesi introduced me to Kenny Bush, the equipment man. Kenny took me over to a small room that had an entire wall filled with shoeboxes. I remember having seen Larry Bowa in a *Sports Illustrated* article at the time of the opening of Veterans Stadium, wearing those red Adidas shoes. When Kenny asked me, "What size you wear, Mike?" I thought I'd died and gone to heaven. Bushy even gave me two pairs, one for artificial turf and one for grass.

I suited up and went out to the field to join in the pregame workout. I took batting practice with the nonregulars—Joe Lis, Oscar Gamble, Byron Browne, and Roger Freed (number 20)—then infield at short with Larry Bowa. (I inherited number 20 in the 1972 offseason after Roger was released.) I was nervous, but confident. I was pumped. I'd been drilled over and over in college on the fundamentals of defense, and I believed I was as good as anyone. A former Ohio University infielder named Terry Harmon was on the Phillies, and he made me feel right at home, actually turning the double play with me. Infield could have gone on for hours; I wouldn't have cared. I couldn't feel the turf beneath my feet.

Afterward, I changed back into street clothes and went up with my dad to watch the game from the owner's box. We repeated this schedule over the next two days; I signed my contract; and then on Sunday management offered me a proposition. The team was going to Reading for an exhibition the next day, and Larry Bowa wasn't feeling good. They asked if I could stay over and take Larry's place at short. *Did I hear that right?* My father and I could stay over, we could travel with the team to Reading, and *I could play shortstop for the big club.* Can you believe that? The last game I'd played was in a college tournament, and now I'm in a big league lineup! Who do you think was the only player thrilled to be in Reading on an off day? And here's the kicker: We win the game, 2–1, on a ninth-inning home run by . . . *Michael Jack Schmidt of Dayton, Ohio!*

Looking back, I don't know where it all came from. (Well, that's not true. I believe God has a predestined plan for us all.) But I always seemed to have had a knack for playing well in special games.

Take the time Paul Owens, the Phillies farm director back then, traveled to OU to see me play. That day I hit a long home run, stole a base, went from first to third on a single, and threw a runner out at first on a ball deep in the hole at short. In other words, I did just about everything a prospect could do—except maybe pitch a couple of shutout innings in relief—at exactly the right time in front of exactly the right audience. Had I done all that the game before or the game after, I might never have ended up in Philadelphia.

Originally, I was scheduled to go to Class A ball following the Reading exhibition game. But that plan was scrapped when I homered in the ninth inning to win the game. That at-bat, and my overall play throughout the weekend, impressed the brass enough for them to start me out on the Class AA Reading team, saving me a whole year in the minors. Who knows what my fate might have been had I been sent to Spartanburg? Who knows what my fate might have been had I been drafted by the Orioles? Who knows what my fate might have been had Paul Owens not picked that one day to see me play college ball? What if my dad had accepted Tony's first offer—that is, the one without the offer to go to Philadelphia to work out with the Phillies?

I thank the good Lord for choosing this plan for me.

When I joined the Reading Phillies after a road game in Elmira, New York, I found my new teammates showering in shifts in the visiting team clubhouse. The "clubhouse" was really only a run-down shack below the stands. The floor of the shack was flooded. My college locker room had been much bigger, much better, much cleaner. It was at this time I realized that I'd led a very sheltered life up until then. I was on my own now, in a world where guys had been scratching for several years to get to this level. And I was scared.

What in the world had I gotten myself into?

That first year in the minors was pretty rocky. I did become friends with Bob Boone, who was moved from third base to catcher, so the shortstop could move over to third and make room for me. But otherwise, that year was a struggle. I didn't get along well with the other guys on the team. They still looked at me as a cocky college kid who had been handed a job. Eventually, I became the team whipping boy. For the most part, I just took it. The way I played, there wasn't much else I could do: .230, 7 HR, 30 RBI in half a season.

Welcome to professional baseball, kid. That pitch you can't hit? We call it a "slider."

Then came Instructional League in the fall, and minor league camp the following spring, and on to . . . *Triple A?* Goodness knows, I sure didn't deserve to go up to Triple A based on my half season in Double A. I learned only much later that Granny Hamner, one of the 1950 Whiz Kids and now a minor league instructor, had been my champion in the Phillies organization, pushing to have me assigned to Triple A in 1972. Fortunately for me, Granny convinced minor league boss Paul Owens to send me to Eugene.

So I reported to the Eugene Emeralds of the Pacific Coast League. Vuk was there; he hadn't made the big club. They moved him to second so I could play third, and he wasn't exactly thrilled about it. We both struggled early, so at first the move didn't look so good for either of us. Fortunately, we both eventually adapted.

I'll always remember our first trip to Albuquerque to play the Dodgers, perennial PCL champions. Tommy Lasorda was their manager. Behind the plate was an old Dayton adversary, Steve Yeager, who signed with the Dodgers as I was going off to college. They had Tom Paciorek, Davey Lopes, Joe Ferguson, Doug Rau, Ron Cey, and a bunch of other guys on the verge of going to the majors. They were *loaded*. Well, we beat them six straight times, and I had a fantastic series, offensively and defensively. (To this day, Lasorda remembers that series like it was yesterday and replays it for me every time I see him.)

Following the final game, we're all in the visitors' clubhouse getting ready to return to the hotel, when our manager, Andy Seminick, hands me a $20 bill and whispers in my ear, "Go buy yourself a steak, son. You deserve it." Today, $20 won't buy you much of a steak, but back then it did. For me, a young kid trying to fit in where he probably didn't belong, I'll cherish that moment forever.

Then, about a month into the season, Andy decided that moving Vuk back to third might help get him going. He asked me, "Schmidt, you ever play second?" I said sure, sure, I've played second before. I lied. Never did. Maybe messing around in practice, a ground ball, or occasionally turning a double play. But I had never taken one ground ball at second in a professional game. So now I'm a second baseman in Triple A.

Moving to second took the pressure off my hitting because, for once, I totally stopped thinking about what to do at the plate. I focused 100 percent on playing second. (Heck, I had to—I'd never played the position.) So naturally I started hitting like a fool, using right field, and hitting the breaking ball. I ended up at .296, with 95 RBI and 26 home runs. I was first-team all-PCL. I had a great year in Triple A, and I was waiting for the call to join the Phillies when rosters were expanded in September.

Near the tail end of my great season in Eugene, I reinjured my left knee. So instead of reporting to the Vet, I checked into a hospital in Philadelphia. Remember my two knee operations in high school? Add on a minor clean-out operation after my year at Reading. That means now, two weeks shy of my twenty-third birthday, I was looking at knee operation number four. As you might imagine, baseball organizations don't take a thing like that casually. They start thinking that maybe they have damaged goods on their hands. I was worried. And I'm pretty sure the Phillies were worried.

Now stepping to the plate, Dr. John Royal Moore, the Phillies doctor and, at the time, a legendary orthopedic surgeon in Philadelphia. Dr. Moore was the James Andrews of his day in sports medicine. At least I was going to be in good hands. So there I am, all prepped for knee surgery, when Dr. Moore comes in for a pre-op conference. We talk a little, he manipulates my leg, and he looks at the X-rays. And then he walks me out into the hallway. "Mike," he says, "take a three-point stance and fire out like you were a split end." I do it. There are the two of us, me and this eighty-year-old doctor in OR scrubs, running and stopping, running and stopping down the hospital hallway. Finally he says, "If you can do that, you don't need surgery. Get outta here, get on back to the Vet and start rehabbing." Three days later, on September 16, 1972, I hit my first home run in the major leagues, a three-run shot off a Montreal left-hander named Balor Moore to beat the Expos.

You've got to be good to play in the big leagues, but you've also got to be lucky. Not getting drafted by the Orioles. Hitting a home run to win the first game I ever played in a Phillies uniform. Having Granny Hamner as a champion in the Phillies organization. Being spared a fourth knee operation at the eleventh hour.

Right time, right place.

God's plan.

I wasn't ready for the big leagues. My good year in Triple A had earned me the September call-up in 1972, but after only a year and a half in the minors, I wasn't ready. You need to understand that the Pacific Coast League, back then, was probably not as tough as the AA Eastern League where I started and flopped in 1971. But fortunately—for me, at least—the Phillies, who hadn't had a winning season since 1967, had nothing to lose, so they opened the door for me. That's how I found myself at third base in the big leagues coming out of spring training in 1973.

Willing? You bet. But ready? That's another story.

I always tend to lump together my call-up in 1972 and my rookie year in 1973. Basically this was a time before I became me. What I mean is that I was a raw talent, with little direction, surviving on a big home run here and there, but with no consistency at all. And I was generally clueless.

My rookie year got off with a resounding thud when, in one of the final spring games, Tony Perez grounded a ball over the third base bag, I dove for it, landed hard, and dislocated my left shoulder. My arm was actually coming out of the front of my shoulder until trainer Don Seger rolled it back into the socket. You ain't seen nothing until you look down and see your arm coming out the front of your shoulder. So, as the team left for Opening Day up North, I stayed in Florida to heal and rehab.

You can imagine how pumped I was when I finally got to start the season. Now multiply that by ten for how I felt the first time I stepped in against Bob Gibson.

Bob Gibson! I had watched this guy dominate hitters for fifteen years. I had owned and cherished his baseball card for ten years. And now, in only the second game of my rookie year, I was standing in the batter's box, looking out at the legend himself. Was I a little uneasy? You could say so.

My first two times at bat, I hacked and flinched and lunged at every nasty slider and high heater Gibson threw me. Somehow, in my third time up, with the score 1–1 in the bottom of the ninth, Gibson put a 2–1 slider low and away, just where he wanted it, and I reached out and hooked a fly down the left field line that cleared the fence for a home run to win the game.

Where on God's green earth did that come from? I circled the bases to a standing ovation, and as I rounded third Mr. Gibson was making his way toward the third base line on his way to the dugout. I didn't know what to do, so I slowed my home run trot to let him pass in front of me.

The next time I faced Gibson, I lucked a cue shot off the end of the bat up the middle for an RBI single. You can guess the postscript to this story. The third time I faced him, he drilled me in the shoulder on the first pitch. Everybody on both benches knew that was coming. Don't you think someone could have warned me? Reaching over the plate to hook a good slider for a home run against Bob Gibson was a no-no, especially from a rookie.

Welcome to the big leagues, kid.

Near the end of my rookie year, I'm leaking oil, big time. Going into the final days, I'm hitting about .204, .205, struggling with all my might to stay above .200. I have 18 homers, but I'm playing so poorly that I'm only in the lineup against left-handers and the occasional B-grade right-hander. Well, when we go to St. Louis for a three-game series, Cesar Tovar, the guy I'm platooning with, decides he's not going to play because of an ongoing contract squabble he's involved in with Phillies management. So now I have to play, and guess who's pitching for the Cardinals in the second game? That's right: Bob Gibson. I'd gone 0–2 the day before, but I was still above .200 for the year. Gibson tacks on an 0–3, which sets up an 0–4 the next day, giving me an 0–9 for the series, which drops my final BA to . . . .196.

Now, Gibson wasn't the only reason I dropped below the .200 mark—he was only responsible for the 0–3; I took care of the 0–6 on my own—but to this day, I think of that final series against St. Louis as Gibby's Revenge.

When I was a kid, baseball was a simple game. It seemed that way when I was growing up. And now, looking back, it still seems that way. But what about kids today? What's it like for them?

Today's kids feel tremendous pressure to develop as athletes and play on winning teams. Many will put years of tee ball, Little League, high school, and college games under their belt, with parents yelling and screaming like life depended on whether you win or lose. Parents fight for positions for their kids on traveling teams and spend thousands of dollars on private coaching, equipment, tournament fees, and airfare. No one pretends it's about fun for the better players; it's about preparing them for the next level.

Many parents of talented kids see their offspring's athletic prowess as their own ticket to success. Look at those ballplayers on television making millions. Why not my son? He can play. If I can just get him to focus, to work harder, to spend more time on his drills. Sure, not all parents fall into this category, but today there is a definite tendency to push kids very hard, very early.

Look, my parents took me to Little League games, they worked in the concession stand, and they sponsored teams. But they never saw me as a kid destined for stardom, much less their ticket to a life on Easy Street. They wanted me to grow up, go to college, be well rounded, be what I wanted to be. They didn't push me. Baseball for me was never a hyper-competitive, pressure-cooker deal as it so often is for so many kids today.

The nationally televised Little League World Series is a perfect example of how kids are being pushed too fast. They're turned into TV stars at age twelve, getting a dose of the big time before they deserve it or can handle it, and most of their parents are riding the wave. The pressure is enormous, way too much for a preteen to handle. As one child is mugging to the crowd like a big leaguer, another is shown crying in the dugout.

Today's version of me at twenty-one has been to many clinics, played thousands of games, has all the instructional videos, a private hitting coach, and certainly an agent. A high second-round draft pick (which I was) is ready (which I wasn't). He's physically conditioned for what's to come, he's got the money and the expectations and the support structure, and he's mentally trained—everything's unfolding exactly the way he'd expected it would. It's nothing for him to walk into a big league clubhouse. He knows that two, three years from now, he's going to be back for his shot, because the club has all this money invested in him. He's part of the deal from day one. Me, I was a long shot. I figured that first day in the Phillies clubhouse would likely be the last time I ever saw it.

Today's version of Tony Lucadello coming to the house to offer me $25,000 is the agent sitting in the farm director's office with the GM, discussing the parameters of the multimillion-dollar signing bonus and a spot on the forty-man roster. Today's version of me is set for life, without having yet thrown or hit a professional pitch.

Times have changed. Back in the day, I bought a new Corvette with my signing bonus. Today, a high pick could buy a fleet.

2 United, We Stood

Clearwater, Florida: spring training, 1976. Make that spring *no* training, 1976. The owners had locked the players out of camps as the continuing struggle over the basic terms of the eight-year-old Collective Bargaining Agreement between the players and the owners began to get nasty. There was a lot of tension and anger and confusion in the air. Then, shortly after the seventeen-day lockout ended and the camps were opened on March 17, I was asked to meet with Phillies owner Ruly Carpenter. It was a meeting that transformed my life. So, though I did not understand it at the time, would the battle over the CBA.

I'm a union man, a member of the Major League Baseball Players Association. I owe a lot to my union. All ballplayers do. But when I first started in the big leagues, being a member of the MLBPA barely registered on my priority list. Little did I know then how important it would become.

In my early years as a pro, from 1971 through 1975, I had little knowledge of or interest in what the players union was all about. Union matters were something the team player representative, usually one of the smarter pitchers or utility types, managed. I can't even remember who our rep was in those days. Occasionally, he'd get us together to relay information regarding the pension, the focus of all squabbles early on, or to sign or vote on something. Most of the time, we approached these meetings as a boring formality and would have flunked a test on the material afterward.

Back then, the pension plan was very important to players. I'd hear talk about how much "time" a guy had in the game. A player's exact time in the big leagues was important because once you got to a certain number of days, you qualified for the pension plan. It's hard to imagine major league players of today's era worrying about a pension payment of $60,000 a year after they turn sixty. In the early 1970s, however, that was something worth fighting for. During my first season, I do remember hoping I could hang around long enough to qualify for a pension.

True, after an eighteen-year career, I had to be reminded by my financial people that I had a pension coming. When I turn sixty, I'll receive $160,000 a year. (You think the battles of the 1970s weren't worth fighting for?) And yet I doubt that a single player today gives the idea of a pension a second thought. But in the early days, gaining time toward your pension was the first goal of every player, and the owners' annual contribution to that plan was the union's primary concern. After all, before 1976, the owners had almost complete control of us, and our pension was really the only element of our financial relationship with our teams that was even remotely negotiable.

Yet there was a much more important issue looming, a basic freedom that had always been denied. During the early 1970s, the players and the union began to see there might be something we could do about it. To some of you, what follows is going to sound a little like Baseball History 101, given how much the subject has been written about and talked about. But I believe the story's worth retelling because it changed the basic structure of baseball. It set the stage for the contemporary era in America's Game and, in my opinion, opened the door for all that's good—and some things that are admittedly bad—in baseball today.

I'm talking, of course, about free agency.

Throughout the history of major league baseball, each player had in his contract a reserve clause. In its simplest form, the reserve clause meant the player was bound by contract to his team until the team decided to trade or release him. The language stated that the club had the right to renew a player's contract for one year, and one year only, should the two parties be unable to agree on salary, with no signature needed on the contract for it to kick in. Basically, this process could go on forever. The player had no say in the matter. If a team traded a player to another team, the traded player had two choices: report to the new team or quit baseball. Besides a trade, the only way to change teams was to be released, which only happened if a team figured you were washed up and had no further value.

No freedom of movement. No chance, while in your prime, to offer your services to the highest bidder. No bargaining leverage whatsoever.

The players were, literally, wage slaves.

Sound a little bit un-American? Well, since the demise of the old Hollywood studio system, you sure didn't find those kinds of restrictions anywhere else in America. That's because since 1922, Major League Baseball has enjoyed an exemption from the federal antitrust laws. Big league owners didn't have to adhere to employment laws that protected the rights of the worker, including the right to bargain collectively. The owners could run their league as a closed shop, outside the rules. The commissioner, an official hired by and paid by the owners to oversee baseball, was the ultimate arbitrator on all grievances.

To the players, this was simply the way it was. We accepted it because if we didn't, we would be out of a job. Basically, I think most players just felt lucky to be playing the game they loved, in the big leagues, and being paid a decent salary to do it. After all, they figured, things could be a whole lot worse.

To the owners, the "free" movement of players was a scary proposition. If players could move to another team after fulfilling their contracts—the way, say, every other worker in America could do—the owners would lose control of the game. The best players would flock to the wealthiest teams. Salaries would skyrocket. As long as the owners had the reserve clause in place, though, they could control salaries and keep their teams intact. They alone decided how big a piece of the pie the players got. Rewarding players for great years—or not—was strictly their call. Every season players had to re-sign with their current teams, go where they were traded—or go home.

Until, in 1970, one did.

At the end of the 1969 season, the St. Louis Cardinals tried to trade center fielder Curt Flood to the Philadelphia Phillies. Except for eleven games with the Reds in 1956–57, Flood had played his entire twelve-year career in St. Louis, where he'd earned a reputation as one of the best center fielders—if not *the* best—in the league. He was making $90,000 a year, excellent money for those times. Flood supposedly found out about the trade from a reporter, and not from the Cardinals front office. What a way for this to go down, for a man who had given his career to the Cardinals. Flood didn't want to go to Philadelphia. In fact, Flood didn't want to be traded *anywhere*. So he consulted a prominent St. Louis attorney for advice. Facing the end of his career if he didn't quietly accept the trade, and tremendous loss of privacy if he fought it in the courts, Curt nevertheless decided to go to war against baseball's reserve clause.

With financial support from the Major League Baseball Players Association, Curt Flood sued Major League Baseball in federal court (*Flood v. Kuhn*) for violation of federal antitrust laws.

At the time it was unfolding, I don't think I even noticed the Flood case, much less understood its implications. I was caught up in my college life, trying just to make the team at Ohio University. Labor issues in the big leagues were somebody else's problems. Little did I know that how they played out would transform my life. Soon.

The most telling moment of the union meetings on the Flood case came when Dodgers catcher Tom Haller asked Curt if he was doing this because he was black. Curt's reply is in Marvin Miller's book, *A Whole Different Ballgame*:

> I'd be lying if I told you as a black man in baseball I hadn't gone through worse times than my white teammates. I'll also say that, yes, I think that the change in black consciousness in recent years has made me more sensitive to injustice in every area of my life. But I want you to know that what I'm doing here I'm doing as a ballplayer, a major league ballplayer, and I think it is absolutely terrible that we have stood by and watched this situation go on for so many years, and never pulled together to do anything about it. It's improper, it shouldn't be allowed to go any further, and the circumstances are such that, well, I guess this is the time to do something.

Enter Marvin Miller. A former economist for the United Steelworkers of America, Miller had been named executive director of the MLBPA in 1966. He rallied support for Flood among the players. In my opinion, based on his accomplishments as the players' leader in a twenty-year war with the Lords of Baseball, Miller deserves—along with Curt Flood—the title "Father of Modern Baseball." And he deserves to be in the Hall of Fame.

Flood v. Kuhn wound up in the Supreme Court. Rumor had it that the voting by the High Court judges on this case ultimately swung on their loyalties to big American corporations, such as Anheuser-Busch, which owned the Cardinals. In 1972, Chief Justice Warren Burger broke a 4–4 deadlock when he reversed his original vote in favor of Flood to make it 5–3 against him.

Even though Curt Flood lost his Supreme Court case against baseball's reserve clause, he still earned the respect of the players for the way he stood up and fought for what he believed in. To a man, major leaguers saw what could be accomplished with leadership, courage, and, most importantly, a strong union. True to his convictions, Flood had refused to report to Philadelphia in 1970. So then the Cardinals had traded Flood to the Washington Senators. Again Curt had refused to budge. Weary from the trial and public pressure, he took his family away to Denmark. Then, out of the clear blue, Senators owner Bob Short had offered Curt $110,000 to report to Washington in 1971. Curt was hurting financially and decided, after a year and a half away from the game, to come back. But the pressure, the missed time, and sheer wear and tear had taken their toll. Flood retired after thirteen games at the age of thirty-three. He died in 1997 at the age of fifty-nine.

Strengthened by the Flood case, even though it ended in the loss column, the MLBPA called the first labor strike in professional sports history in 1972. The trigger was the owners' unwillingness to increase the pension fund to keep up with the cost of living. The owners were careless. They saw this as a battle against Marvin Miller, not the players, and underestimated the strength of a united

union. They also figured that without the support of the elite players, who had a lot to lose in salary in a strike, and relatively little
to gain by an adjustment in the pension contribution, the MLBPA
would fold like a cheap suit.

They were half right. If guys like Willie Mays, Pete Rose, and
Hank Aaron had not stepped up to say they were behind the union
all the way and refused to play until the union's demands were met,
the MLBPA wouldn't have had a prayer. But the stars stepped up.
The owners caved, and the 1972 season finally got under way thirteen days late, with eighty-six games wiped out. The MLBPA had
won its first major dispute with baseball's ownership, and baseball's
pension plan remains the model of all professional sports. Player confidence in the power of the union and in Miller's leadership soared.

The next paving stone in the players' road to liberation from
the reserve clause came courtesy of Charles Finley, the eccentric
owner of the Oakland A's. Finley and his star pitcher, Catfish Hunter,
had a little side deal: a loan against salary that Finley, chronically
short of cash, called in early. Catfish had to sell some property to
pay him. The next year they had another side deal that involved
a payment to an annuity on Hunter's behalf. Looking for a crack
in the agreement, and without thinking of possible consequences,
Finley defaulted on a payment. Hunter filed a grievance, and an
arbitrator deemed his contract null and void. Hunter thus became
the first "free" player—that is, he was free to offer his services to
any club. At the time Hunter was making $100,000 as the best
big-game pitcher in baseball. Now, following his free agency, he
became the highest-paid athlete in professional sports when the
Yankees signed him for $3.75 million over five years. Who better
than George Steinbrenner to get the ball rolling?

Free agency, a beautiful thing!

From 1972 through 1975, several players tested the "one-year re-
newal" element of the basic players contract: Al Downing (Dodgers),

Bobby Tolan (Padres), Ted Simmons (Cardinals), and the main players, Andy Messersmith (Dodgers) and Dave McNally (Orioles). It seems there was a potential loophole in section 10A, where the contract stated the team could renew a player's contract without the player's signature. Messersmith, under contract to the Dodgers and locked in a dispute with owner Walter O'Malley over a no-trade clause, played the 1975 season without a contract and then sought to sign with the Braves. McNally, traded by the Orioles to the Expos after the 1974 season, played for Montreal in 1975 with an unsigned contract and, because he was planning on retiring and therefore couldn't be hurt by taking a stand, became the other challenger to this rule.

The stage was set: Two prominent players, playing without a signed contract, filed grievances stating that they had been forced to perform without a signed contract. This was a serious test of the basic contractual agreement in place at that time, which stated that a player's contract could be renewed unilaterally without his signature. Correct legal language or not, Miller knew the players' best bet was to subject the dispute to binding arbitration, as they were entitled to do under the Collective Bargaining Agreement.

Think Flood and Hunter caused a stir? This was a bombshell. Veteran arbitrator Peter Seitz ruled on December 23, 1975, that nowhere in section 10A of the player contract did it say a player could be renewed for *more* than one year without his consent. By not consenting to Messersmith's plea for a no-trade clause, and by renewing a contract that Messersmith refused to sign, Walter O'Malley had unwittingly opened the door to free agency in baseball—one that the players, led by Marvin Miller, now walked through.

After Seitz's ruling in the Messersmith and McNally cases, every player contract was now interpreted to say that after one year of service on that contract, the player could elect not to re-sign with the current team and opt for free agency.

This changed the face of baseball forever.

• • •

At the time all this was bubbling up, I was coming off two very good years. I led the league in home runs and slugging percentage in 1974 and finished second in RBI, runs, and total bases. In 1975, after a dismal start, I finished with 38 home runs, again leading the league.

During my rookie year, I was paid the league minimum: $15,500. Then, in the middle of 1974, on a West Coast trip, I was offered a two-year $100,000 deal, effective immediately. Wow! The Phillies were serious about my future, and now I had some serious folding money. It didn't cross my mind at the time that Phillies management might also have been worried about the storm clouds brewing.

The ruling in the Messersmith case triggered a drastic move by the owners: They locked players out of spring training camp preceding the 1976 season. This lockout was prompted by the owners' growing fear that the reserve clause would become history and spell the end of professional baseball as they knew (and ran) it.

Believe me, some players thought the same thing. The current system was all we knew, and the owners' insistence that they had to control the movement of players seemed right—until we got an education from Miller. I didn't even know what "antitrust" meant, let alone that baseball was excluded from the rules that govern all other businesses. I couldn't imagine a player being free to offer services to the highest bidder, like a painter, a lawyer, or an actor. But like most players, I trusted Marvin, his staff, and the player reps. My opinions, and those of most of my teammates, were shaped by these men in the trenches. Deep down, I hoped the owners didn't decide just to fold up the league and go home. Basically, our only choice was to stand united behind Marvin's leadership.

On March 17, Commissioner Bowie Kuhn ordered teams to reopen training camps as soon as possible under an agreement that both sides would negotiate in good faith to rewrite the document governing player-owner relations in the best interests of baseball. It took until July 12 of that year to complete the task. The news was released in Philadelphia during the All-Star break. The new Collective Bargaining Agreement contained many elements, but the essence of it was that after a sixth year in the major leagues, a player could exercise his right to become a free agent by not re-signing with his current club.

Our world had changed. Just how much, we had no idea.

Most of us Phillies didn't want to change teams. In those days, we enjoyed a bond of loyalty among teammates, and with our owner. Maybe not so on other teams, but we were a family. We came up through the minors together, we spent time together, we raised our kids together, we worked out together in the off-season, we struggled to play in Philadelphia together, and we wanted to win together. We had new homes in New Jersey, and kids in school. We had a new stadium, some new faces on the team, and we felt it was a matter of time before we were champions.

I definitely wanted to stay in Philadelphia. Lucky for me, Phillies owner Ruly Carpenter and GM Paul Owens felt the same way.

After spring training resumed in 1976, Ruly Carpenter asked if he could meet with me privately. The meeting took place at my condo in Clearwater. No agent, no lawyers, no GM. Just Ruly and me, man to man. He was ill-at-ease, obviously a bit uncomfortable with what he was getting ready to tell me, no doubt because it was unprecedented. What Ruly was about to do was make me the highest-paid player in National League history.

Ruly explained the circumstances to me like a father, talking to me about things like responsibility and leadership. He said he had discussed this at length with his advisers. To him, he said, I wasn't a commodity that he would just use for a year or two. He wanted me to be the centerpiece of his team for a long time. His offer:

$550,000 per year for six years. Unheard of. I wasn't even a free agent, and the Phillies obviously didn't want me to become one. Going into the 1976 season I would be the highest-paid player in the National League.

It was all a matter of timing, and of the new world baseball was just entering. You see—and I know this sounds immodest, but I also think it's true—I was the best young player in the league at the time. Rather than face my demands in two years, the Phillies decided to bite the bullet early. I was among the first players to reap the fruits of a long, hard, often bitter struggle, the result of which was to have a revolutionary impact on baseball.

For the rest of my career, I was one of the highest-paid players in all of baseball. Sure, Yankee and Angel free agents over the next several years surpassed my numbers, but few in the National League ever did. So I was essentially set for life financially, and free of the pressure to win a raise year to year.

Over the next five years, the Phillies were labeled in the preseason previews as the team to beat in the National League. The Dodgers, Reds, and Pirates did just that from 1976 to 1979, but we were in the thick of the pennant race every season. And in 1980, we won it all.

My point here is that Ruly Carpenter's investment in me back in 1976, and his many investments in my teammates since then, paid off. Our championship in 1980 has been well documented, but the success of the organization as a whole from 1976 through 1983 is the real story. Many who participated in that championship, both on the field and off, are still with the club in some capacity. Far from creating chaos and destroying the organization, free agency helped build it.

Even so, some owners—notably not ours—publicly whined about the rising salaries. (Between 1976 and 1980, the average major league salary rose from $52,300 to $146,500.) They claimed their teams were losing money, that rising salaries and free agency were ruining the competitive balance of baseball. And yet business was booming. Attendance and gate receipts, television and radio revenues, income from concessions, and franchise values all set record highs each year. Everyone benefited. Coaches, trainers, administrators, and even umpires got big bumps in their salaries.

And the players . . . Wow! During this period, the three most notable signings were Reggie Jackson, Yankees (five years, $2.66 million); Pete Rose, Phillies (four years, $3.2 million); and Nolan Ryan, Astros (three years, $3.5 million). Nolan was the first professional athlete to earn more than $1 million per year.

Imagine, a baseball player making *$1 million* a year!

The CBA, with the free agency package as the focal point, had expired and was up for renegotiation in 1980. The players, with years of hearing how the owners were losing money, how the competitive balance was gone, and how the end of the world was near, decided to show solidarity by refusing to play the final seven days of spring training in 1980. The regular season opened on time, but we set a May 23 strike date. This would force the owners to come to the bargaining table in good faith. On the eve of the strike deadline, an agreement was made to table the issue of free agency until the off-season. All other issues were negotiated and agreed upon. The season went on without interruption.

Not so in 1981. Riddled by the daily posturing of various owners and negotiators following the 1980 season, the situation got uglier and uglier. The owners were hell-bent on breaking the union and destroying Marvin Miller. They believed players had too much to risk by striking, and that some of the higher-profile, higher-paid stars would cross the line. Meanwhile, the players set up strike funds, workout locations, and meeting places. A siege mentality developed on both sides of the player-owner line.

The negotiations settled around free agent compensation. The owners wanted a team losing a free agent player to get something substantial in return from the team that signed him. The players wanted to be sure that the compensation would not be so substantial as to inhibit the freedom of player movement.

This time around, the players were considerably more educated on the business side of the game. We knew and appreciated the reality of free movement of players. We were enjoying a much bigger piece of the total revenue pie. The owners claimed they were losing money, but franchise values kept skyrocketing, so we were highly skeptical of their claims. They saw a "compensation payment" for the signing of a free agent as a way to slow things down to a more manageable system. We saw it as an infringement on the operation of a free market.

Both sides dug in their heels.

From Opening Day, a black cloud hung over the 1981 season—and it kept getting blacker. Not a day went by without a labor negotiations issue topping the sports pages. We were ready for the worst, but the Phillies—and I—were playing some of our best baseball. We had the 1980 World Championship under our belts, and believed we would repeat. I had my first NL MVP award and the World Series MVP award. As of June 11, we were in first place, and I was having a great season, leading the majors in home runs (14) and RBI (41). The only thing that could stop us, we figured, was a strike.

Then, on June 13, 1981, the *Philadelphia Inquirer* ran this headline on its front page: FINAL OUT.

Weird, I actually got to spend the next fifty summer days like a normal person. I didn't have to go to the park at three every day. I didn't have to go on road trips. My wife, Donna, and I ate dinner at a normal time. Our kids—Jess, two, and Jonathan, one—were still babies, so my time with the family was as precious as it was extraordinary. There were daily updates available through Bob Boone, our player rep and one of the lead negotiators. And I'll never forget going down to a local ballfield with Tug McGraw to play catch, run, and try to stay in baseball shape. And I got a kick out of a part-time gig that lasted for the duration of the strike: weekend sports anchor for the local CBS TV affiliate. But most of all, I'll never forget the waiting.

The owners blinked first. Baseball lost 712 total games in 1981, including the All-Star Game, but the players kept the compensation rider out of free agency. Also, players were credited with fifty days of service time toward their pensions, and the Collective Bargaining Agreement was extended through 1984. The owners flat-out miscalculated the strength of the union and its leadership. Their plan to split the union and abolish free agency failed. Player salary losses during that strike came to something like $35 million, but the sacrifice was worth it: over the next nine years, total combined major league payroll went from $121 million to $388 million.

The All-Star Game—we finally played it on August 9—kicked off the return of baseball in 1981. We packed 72,086 fans into Cleveland's old Municipal Stadium, the biggest crowd in All-Star Game history. I won it for the National League with a home run off Rollie Fingers. It was good to be back.

To compensate for the lost games, the 1981 season was divided into two halves, with the first-half winner playing the second-half winner in a mini-series, before the League Championship Series. We won the first half, but lost the mini-series against the Expos, who then lost in the NLCS against the Dodgers, who'd beaten the Astros to get there. The Cardinals, who had the best overall record in the National League, didn't get into the playoffs.

The clinching game of what would become the "first half," against Houston, was one I'll never forget. Pete Rose needed two hits to pass Stan Musial as the National League's career leader in hits, and Nolan Ryan was on the mound for the Astros. In his first at-bat, Pete singled sharply to left to tie Musial. The sold-out crowd in the Vet went nuts. Pete's next three at-bats were the stuff that today would be opening highlights on *ESPN SportsCenter*. Ryan struck out Pete three straight times. Rose, like a boxer who had been taken apart by his opponent, walked away from the plate after the third K and tipped his hat toward the mound. That gesture had enormous hidden meaning to the players on both benches: With the lockout looming, we knew that could have been Pete's last at-bat for the season.

The 1981 season was also important to me for personal reasons. In 102 games, I hit 31 home runs and drove in 91 runs to win my second MVP—and once again free agency surfaced in my life. Make that loomed. My 1976 contract was to take me into 1982, at which time I could test the market. I was the 1980 equivalent of Alex Rodriguez. If I became a free agent, I was a lock to become the highest-paid player in sports history.

But I had no interest in uprooting my family from our beautiful home and our friends, and leaving an organization where I had built lifelong friendships. Yes, Philadelphia is a tough town, and there were hard times, but it was my baseball home, and the Phillies were accommodating. Following the 1981 season, my negotiating team of Arthur Rosenberg and Paul Shapiro hammered out the largest contract to date in baseball. Over the next six years, I would receive $11.42 million.

Can you imagine what I might have gotten as a free agent?

Well, it's 2006, and we know the effect free agency has had on salaries. Many players today make well over my career salary total in one year. The average salary in 1981 was $196,500. In 2005, it was $2.63 million. I'm often asked if I regret not playing today. People say, "Can you imagine what you'd be making?" My answer is always the same: Hank Aaron, Willie Mays, and Frank Robinson all made around $100,000 in their best years, so what do I have to complain about? Everything's relative. I played in the best baseball era ever, in my opinion, and I reaped the fruits of the early years of free agency.

Is there a downside? Yes, I think there is. Once upon a time, players spent most of their careers with one team. Sure, there were trades now and then, but most players on most teams came up through the organization and stayed with it until they left the game. Fans developed a bond with "their" players. Think about the Dodgers of the 1950s. Or the Yankees of the 1960s. Or the Phillies of the 1970s.

Free agency changed that. Players could now sell their services to the highest bidder. And they did—tentatively at first, but rapidly increasing to what we see today: an annual migration of household names to more affluent households.

Team A responds to the threat of losing a star player to free agency by trading him to Team B the year before he can declare. Team B knows it's for only one season, but figures the "rental" is worth it if he helps put them into the postseason. Good for Team A? Maybe. Good for Team B? Maybe. Good for the star player? Absolutely. Good for player-fan loyalty? You tell me.

Don't get me wrong. I am 100 percent in favor of free agency. I was a direct beneficiary of Marvin Miller's revolution even though I never was a free agent myself. Free agency has been great for the players and—I believe—for the overall quality of the game.

But look at a player like Gary Sheffield. Terrific hitter. Good fielder. A huge asset for every team he's played for. And there's the rub. In eighteen major league seasons, Gary Sheffield has played for *six* teams. Up until free agency, the only guys who played for that many teams were spare parts, journeymen who got thrown into trades to make the deals work. Sheffield's a *star*—and he's shone in half a dozen different uniforms.

Free agency has been great for Gary Sheffield. But what about kids in Milwaukee, San Diego, Miami, Los Angeles, and Atlanta who first fell in love with the game because of him? He was *their* hero. And then, suddenly, he belonged to somebody else.

(At least kids in New York who got turned on to baseball the last couple of years by Gary Sheffield as a New York Yankee aren't likely to see him move on to, say, the Mets and break their hearts. After all, Gary's thirty-eight.)

Curt Flood never reaped any reward for his stand against Major League Baseball. He understood that what he was doing was for the players of the future. I wonder how many of today's players know the story of Curt Flood? Or what Andy Messersmith and Dave McNally did for them? Or the risks the early leaders of the MLB-PA ran in standing up to the owners? Or the huge role played by Marvin Miller in transforming baseball—and our lives—by ending business as usual? These men made possible my salary, my security, and all that followed.

Their story, and the story of how free agency in baseball came about, should be required reading for all athletes in professional sports today, too many of whom take their financial bonanza for granted. The salaries of athletes competing in the major sports today are direct consequences of the courage of those who fought baseball owners in the 1970s.

Conduct a poll of athletes in the big four professional team sports today. Ask them just one question: Who was Curt Flood?

How many do you think could correctly identify him as the man who sacrificed his career to make theirs possible?

3 The Best of Times

My entire rookie season was a nightmare. Only a sacrifice bunt in my third at-bat saved me from striking out five times one night against Tom Seaver and the Mets. I could hit a fastball, but that was about it. I managed 18 home runs and 52 RBI, but I hit .196 and struck out 136 times in 367 at-bats. That's more than one K every three AB, if you do the math. (And believe me, I did, over and over.)

I also spent most of the year in manager Danny Ozark's doghouse. He took to calling me "Dumb Dutchman" because I wouldn't listen to his batting tips and was a general pain in the butt all year.

My first year was a complete bust. Looking ahead to 1974, I was determined to find a way to stay in the big leagues.

In those days, it was standard procedure for a prospect to play winter ball for more experience. So off I went a couple of weeks after the 1973 season to Caguas, Puerto Rico. As you can imagine, I was a little short on confidence when I reported.

Only people who know me well understand what I went through

to become a hitter. I never met anybody in my entire major league career who was as deeply into the mental side of hitting as I was. I always needed a specific, mechanical element—a swing thought, to use a golf term—to focus on to get me through an at-bat. I was the Nick Faldo of baseball. See ball/hit ball? No way. To me, that would be like being lost in the woods without a compass.

So it's not surprising that the swing thought I tried out in Puerto Rico washed away the bad taste of my .196 rookie year. It surfaced in an at-bat against Pedro Borbon, who was coming off a terrific season with the Reds (11–4, 2.16 ERA). I went to the plate with one idea in my head: Swing softly, under control, on balance. Just lay the bat squarely on the ball; don't try to add a little something extra on the point of contact.

Boom! I hit a rocket off the left field wall.

That one swing—and one approach to hitting—kick-started my career as a power hitter.

Despite my awful rookie season, I was still starting at third base for the Philadelphia Phillies coming out of spring training in 1974. For just how long, though, was up in the air, because I'd had a major confrontation with Ozark, who gave me an ultimatum: Change my hitting approach or go back to the minors. The day he threatened me, I blustered right back: "I'm not changing, so go ahead and send me to Triple A." Cocky? On the outside, sure. But inside I was scared witless. All I knew was that I was going to "swing softly" and put the ball in play.

That's exactly what I did from Opening Day, which I capped with a game-winning homer off Mets closer Tug McGraw. At the All-Star break, I had 19 HR and 67 ribbies, leading the league in both categories, and I became an All-Star for the first time, setting a record for the most write-in votes in history. A young intern at a local radio station, Howard Eskin, headed the write-in campaign.

Much later, I got to know Howard, who became a great friend; he richly deserves the title "king" of sports talk radio in Philly.

I ended up leading the NL in home runs (36) and slugging percentage (.546), and drove in 116 runs. The same guy who hit .196 the year before, the guy who should have been sent back to AAA, was a candidate for the NL MVP. From the worst hitter in baseball to one of the best—in one year.

Things took a good turn for the team, as well. The Phillies had made a key acquisition over the winter by trading for second baseman Dave Cash of the Pirates. "A.C."—short for Always Cool—became my mentor. He bubbled with praise for Larry Bowa and me, and we both ate it up. We were called the 10–20–30 Club—numbers 10, 20, 30—second, third, short. The Phillies had the best infield in baseball, and we knew it.

The Phillies made a move in 1974: After three straight seasons in the cellar, we finished third in the NL East and sauntered into 1975 expecting to contend. Unfortunately, the *swing e-a-s-y* contact stroke left me at some point in the off-season and never even said goodbye. The first half of 1975, I was flat-out awful.

But then something happened that made me come alive in the second half. Make that some*one*: Dick Allen.

For more than a decade, since his Rookie of the Year season for the Phillies in 1964 (when he was known as Richie), Allen had been one of the most consistent sluggers in the game, first for the Phils, then, later, for the Cardinals, the Dodgers, and the White Sox. In December 1974, the White Sox traded him to the Braves—or tried to. Dick, who lived on a horse farm outside Philadelphia, decided to retire instead of report. A seven-time All-Star who had led the AL in homers two of the preceding three years, Allen was, at age thirty-two, out of the game, raising horses outside Philly, an easy drive from the Vet.

Always eccentric, Allen was a legend in Philadelphia, where

the fans loved him. Another Phillies legend, Richie Ashburn—star center fielder of the 1950 Whiz Kids, Hall of Famer, longtime Phillies announcer—evidently got wind that Cash and I, two players Allen evidently admired, might be able to persuade Dick to return to baseball to play first base for us. So one off day Ashburn, Cash, and I drove out to Perkasie to meet with Dick. I'll never forget playing horse—with a basketball, not a Thoroughbred—on an old hoop hanging in his barn while we talked about how well he'd fit in on the Phillies. Dick said he'd think about it. Shortly thereafter, he and the Phillies worked out a deal, and after a few days of BP at the Vet, Dick was ready.

At that time we badly needed a hitter in the five hole who would command enough respect to force the other team to pitch to Greg Luzinski. Dick became that man—and more. I had another mentor, someone who decided to put on that Phillies uniform for one reason: to help us understand what it took to win. We responded. I came alive under Dick's and A.C.'s watch in the second half of 1975 to finish with 38 home runs and again lead the league. We finished second, one step closer to the top.

(Dick once referred to me as "the baddest white boy" he ever played with. I took it as the highest of compliments.)

Another huge plus from 1975, one that had a profound impact on my life and on the team, was a trade with the Giants that brought us Garry Maddox. Garry had played for a short time in the Pacific Coast League the same year I did, just long enough to become a PCL legend before being called up by the Giants. I saw him just once, when he returned to Phoenix after his call-up and watched a game from the stands. Everybody knew about his lightning speed. (Garry was the fastest man from home to second I ever saw—no more than fifteen steps, I swear!) With his full beard and Afro, Garry was a little scary to people who didn't know him. He had an aura about him. At a team meeting just before he arrived,

Ozark explained that Garry was a quiet man, with a tough personal history related to Vietnam, and that he had a skin condition on his neck that prohibited him from shaving, so our no-beard policy was waived. (Nice move, Garry.)

Later, some newspaper guy hung the nickname "Secretary of Defense" on him, and it was a perfect fit. Garry was the greatest center fielder of his era, maybe the greatest ever. Somebody else— Ralph Kiner, I think—once summed up Garry's skills this way: "Two-thirds of the earth is covered by water. The other third is covered by Garry Maddox."

More important, Garry became a mentor and a close friend, and we shared in something far larger than baseball. We grew close as we searched for our spiritual lives together, and as we did charity work in the community. He was—still is—the most unselfish person I've ever met. That intimidating, mysterious Vietnam vet I saw in the stands in Phoenix back in 1972 would become my best friend in the game.

The Bicentennial season, 1976, was a great time to be in Philadelphia, but the highlight of the year for me came in Chicago. Since Wrigley Field became the Cubs' home in 1916, every National League power hitter has loved road trips to Chicago. I was no exception. People call Wrigley the "Friendly Confines," and those confines are especially friendly to hitters who put a little air under the ball. The first thing I used to do every morning when we played a series in Chicago was to look out my hotel window, find a flag, and check which way the wind was blowing.

Hot summer day, wind blowing out toward Lake Michigan? Let's play two!

I never think about Chicago and Wrigley Field without recalling a league-wide ritual that proves once and for all, if proof is needed, that there's a lot of little boy in the men who play baseball for a living. On game days, the team bus from our downtown hotel to Wrigley always went up Michigan Avenue, past a giant equestrian statue of a General John Logan (a Union hero at the Battle of Vicksburg during the Civil War, I later learned). Every time—I mean, *every* time—we rode by, some guy on the bus would yell out, "Don't look at the horse's balls! Don't look at the horse's balls!" And then the whole bus would turn it into a chant: *Don't look at the horse's balls! Don't look at the horse's balls!* It was supposed to be bad luck. Well, I'm ridiculously superstitious, so you can bet I never looked.

Our first road trip to Chicago in 1976 came early in the season. We'd gotten off to a slow start, in part because I couldn't buy a hit. Before we headed out to the dugout for the National Anthem, Dick Allen asked me to hang back with him. He told me it looked to him like I was pressing, not having any fun on the field, and trying to carry the entire load. He suggested I do nothing but have fun on the field that day. I figured okay, why not? After all, if a hitter's in a slump, he'll listen to anybody with a plan.

Anyway, Dick and I went out on the field and tried to have some fun. Between innings, he'd throw me lob passes with the ball like a quarterback. In the dugout, we'd horse around, joke, laugh. It took my mind away from results, and I quickly loosened up. It also probably helped that we fell behind 12–1!

Loose is good; getting a hit is better. And that's what I did in my second at-bat, an RBI single. Then in my third at-bat, I hit a home run to left off Rick Reuschel. Next time up, I hit another home run off Reuschel. (Hey, we're coming back! And I'm having fun!) Fifth at-bat, now facing Mike Garman: A long home run to center brings us to just one run down (13–12). (Now I'm *really* having fun!) And then, sixth time up, with Rick's brother Paul Reuschel now pitching, *bingo!*

Phillies hold on to win, 18–16, in ten innings.

Not a bad day at the office, all things considered: 5 for 6, 8 RBI, 4 HR in a comeback win—all because I didn't look at the horse's balls!

(Yes, now that you mention it: The wind *was* blowing out.)

Just fifteen players in history have hit four homers in a game, and I'm proud to be in the group. But I'm doubly pleased by what that special day in the Friendly Confines started: a blistering hot streak in which we won 50 of our next 68, sending us to a 101–61 record and the division title. Boone, Cash, Bowa, Luzinski, and I made the All-Star team that summer, and we got a huge standing ovation when we were introduced at the game played, that Bicentennial year, in Philadelphia.

Our run of Eastern Division championships began in 1976, and so did our run of NLCS failures. We lost to the Big Red Machine—Rose, Morgan, Bench, Perez, Foster, & Co.—but who didn't that year? Still, 1976 was a stellar year for the organization, the first in a stretch during which we were one of the elite teams in baseball. The Phillies had become the Dodgers of the NL East—a team full of young All-Stars just learning how to win.

In 1977, we picked up exactly where we'd left off. We were the team to beat in the NL East. We won the division in Chicago on September 27, my twenty-eighth birthday. Then we went on to meet the Dodgers in the 1977 NLCS.

No icing on this cake: the Dodgers whacked us three games to one and sent us home for the winter.

My nonbaseball world changed dramatically in the winter of 1977–78. Several of my teammates—Garry Maddox, Bob Boone, Terry Harmon—and friends from other teams (Bobby Jones, Doug Collins) and our wives became involved in a Bible study group led by a local biblical scholar and the president (1971–2001) of the Association of Baptists for World Evangelism, Wendell Kempton.

This was a life-changing experience for all of us. We took turns hosting the study group at one another's homes, where we studied the practical applications of the Bible, learned about the power of prayer, and shared in each other's search for spiritual truth. On January 9, 1978, I surrendered. I was convinced there was no other way to go through life than with a personal relationship with God, as laid out in the Bible. From that day of acceptance and rebirth, I have had a clear view of who's really in charge, of my relationship to Him, of the power of that connection, and of the eternal hope that accompanies it.

To this day, Wendell Kempton remains the most influential non-sports-related person in all of our lives.

Unfortunately—or fortunately, depending on your point of view—this new joy in my life became big news in Philadelphia. One tabloid printed the headline SCHMIDT FINDS RELIGION in big bold black letters on its back page. The story was written by a young woman with whom I'd spent considerable time explaining why and how I came to this spiritual commitment, and why it would make everything about me better, including my game. As a new Christian, you find yourself excited and eager to share your newfound spirit with others. It's part of His plan; you just can't help it. Unfortunately—or fortunately, as Wendell said at the time—God used me to share His power with an entire city in a single headline.

To this day I'm grateful for that period in my life. I always will have strong Christian beliefs, a basis for prayer and forgiveness, and a clear vision of eternity, all valuable assets as I grow old. This is the most cherished takeaway from my baseball career.

Would this newfound spiritual connection help me lead the Phillies to a World Championship? No. God had other plans.

The 21 home runs and 78 RBI I finished with in 1978 weren't my style, but winning the division was. Once again, we faced the Dodgers in the NLCS. And once again Lopes, Cey, Garvey, Baker, & Co. prevailed, three games to one.

We were crushed. We couldn't win when it counted. And I couldn't hit in the big games. My postseason output over three years was 8 hits in 44 at-bats. My rookie season all over again, this time compressed into eleven games.

Life was put into perspective, though, just before Christmas. Donna and I had been told that it was doubtful we would be able to have children. But after two years of meditation and prayer, we were gifted with beautiful little Jessica Rae Schmidt, born on December 19. She was our Christmas miracle.

As you can imagine, my life changed in a big way.

Following a long and highly publicized tour as the star free agent of 1978, Pete Rose turned down several better offers to play in Philadelphia. His ongoing friendship with Luzinski and Bowa probably was the main reason for his choice. Phillies owner Bill Giles, looking for something to get this team over the playoff hump, decided Pete was the answer. The team needed an emotional leader, like Dave Cash in the early 1970s. We needed a guy we all respected, a guy who offered a different perspective, someone from another team who was a blue-chip player. Great teams have leaders at the top of the order who understand how valuable getting on base is, and no one understands this better than Pete.

Once Pete was on board, there was no off-season talk around town about us tanking in the 1978 playoffs. It was all about Pete coming to Philly and what he brought to the party. Fans who hated him as a Red now loved him as a Phillie. Pete hit .331 and played every game—with almost 60 hits in the month of September after he was served divorce papers! I was a major benefactor of his big year, driving in 114 runs, and we developed a friendship that would eventually push me to new heights as a player.

Pete lived for baseball. He was first to the park every day. He'd be sitting at his locker or in the middle of the room, almost like he was waiting for each guy to get there. He'd kid all of us about something we did the previous day, or something we were wearing, anything to get a laugh. He was the first guy I ever saw who slapped hands with everyone, for any reason. He kept us thinking positively, and he challenged us to keep up with him.

Pete never let it show, but he was going through tough personal times. He was estranged from his wife, and he was also dealing with what we know now was a gambling problem. At the time, nobody in the Phillies clubhouse had any idea that he had a gambling problem, much less any idea how large it would become. Often we'd sit around the clubhouse and discuss point spreads of football and basketball games. We knew he bet but never gave a thought to it becoming serious.

But we also knew Pete was going to get his hits, no matter what the circumstances, and that he made us a much better team. And that's what mattered.

Something else began to matter to all of baseball: Trouble between players and owners was brewing again. In early April 1980, the players voted 967–1 to cancel the final week of spring training as a show of solidarity. (Jerry Terrell of Minnesota was the lone dissenter, for religious reasons.) We set a strike date of May 23. Serious business? Sure, but it also offered an opportunity for some serious fun, like for kids when school gets cancelled. Tug McGraw, Steve Carlton, and I chartered a forty-five-foot sport fishing boat that we called home for a week. It came from St. Petersburg and docked in the Clearwater Marina, where we partied for the final week of spring training. We worked out each morning at a local field—throwing, running, and hitting. But the remainder of the day was spent on the water. If all spring training camps were like that, I might still be playing.

That little spring break turned out to be just what we needed to get off on the right foot in 1980. We played great ball from the git-go, but we weren't the only ones. Our nemesis in 1980, and again in 1981, was the Montreal Expos: Andre Dawson, Tim Raines, Gary Carter, Steve Rogers, and that gang gave us all we could handle. We battled them and the Pirates all season, as the NL East title came down to the last week, a week I'll never forget. With a four-game series at home against the Cubs and a three-game weekend season finale in Montreal facing us, we were a half game behind the Expos. They had all six games at home—three with St. Louis and then us.

Things started out terribly for me, but not on the field. I was informed over the weekend that my grandmother Schmidt, seventy-eight, had passed away. Grandma Me (as my sister, Sally, and I called her) was like a mother to us. She worked in a local factory called The Dayton Pump at the same little bench for more than thirty years, lived alone in a little apartment in north Dayton, and *really* lived for her grandchildren. It seemed every weekend of my life as a kid was spent with her. She pitched to me, took me to Little League games, and made the best fried chicken and chocolate cake with caramel icing you could imagine. She loved Pete Rose and had a poster of him on the back of her bedroom door so she could tailor my high school uniforms to fit like his. (Tight, not baggy like today.) I really believe she was watching the playoff run from above—with a big smile at seeing Pete and me on the same team.

After traveling to Dayton for the funeral, I returned in time to get in the lineup for the series opener against the Cubs, a key game in our stretch drive. The first game was decided in the bottom of the fifteenth, when, after I had left the winning run on third, Garry Maddox drove it in. His hit may have been the biggest of our final week, as we went on to sweep the Cubs and set up the final showdown with the Expos.

Having to win two of three in Montreal to win the NL East was a giant task, and we couldn't use Carlton, who'd pitched in the Cubs series. I remember doing something I never did before or after. Walking down the street after lunch that Friday with my old buddy Tim McCarver, I told him I felt good about this series and we had nothing to worry about. Something told me that I was about to take over, which was not like me, but I felt it.

Turns out I was on the money. We won the first game 2–0 on my sacrifice fly and forty-seventh home run. The Saturday game was delayed by rain for two hours, but who was watching the clock? In the eleventh inning, I hit my forty-eighth home run, the shot heard all the way back in Philly.

It was a 2–0 fastball, out over the plate, off Stan Bahnsen. Pete was on second, first base was open, and Don McCormack, who had never hit in the big leagues, was on deck. And yet somehow Expos manager Dick Williams allowed Bahnsen to pitch to me. That homer was the defining moment in my career to that point and remains one of the greatest moments in Phillies history.

Tug McGraw—"Neighbor," as we called each other, God rest his soul—pitched five shutout innings in those two wins, struck out nine, and closed out each game. His pitching made me a hero.

I needed that series. Philly fans were split on whether I was a money player. It hurt me to know they doubted me, but personally I doubted myself, too. I hadn't hit well in the postseason, and the fans hadn't forgotten it. I needed to step up. Fortunately, I did. In our final six wins of the 1980 regular season, four against the Cubs and two over the Expos, I went 10 for 25 with 4 home runs and 7 RBI. My home runs tied one of the final four games and won the other three.

The 1980 NLCS against Houston, with all but the first game going into extra innings, was one of the greatest playoff series in baseball history, ranking right up there with 1986 (Mets–Astros) and 2004 (Red Sox–Yankees). I had a poor series, and in the final game I left the tying run on third with one out in the eighth. That would have been a ball-and-chain I'd have carried, with the help of Philly fans, for a long, long time, had it not been for Del Unser.

After splitting the first two games at the Vet, we went into Houston needing two of three to win the pennant. We were looking at Joe Niekro, Vern Ruhle, and Nolan Ryan. The Astrodome was busting at the seams, sold out every game, 45,000 strong, and the noise was deafening. We lost game three against Niekro 1–0 in eleven innings, but won game four in ten innings, 5–3.

Now all that was left was to beat Nolan Ryan in game five.

Imagine being down to the greatest game closer of our time by three runs going into the eighth inning, in his park, with 45,000 screaming fans making it almost impossible to think. Now imagine the greatest inning in Phillies history beginning to unfold . . .

Bowa leads off against Ryan with a single up the middle. Then Boonie singles up the middle. First and second, nobody out. Greg Gross lays down a perfect drop bunt single. Next up, Pete Rose. I'll never forget Pete screaming at Ryan as he walks to the plate: "You ain't getting me out!" Rose walks to score Bowa. Keith Moreland pinch-hits for Bake McBride and drives in a run with a ground ball to second. That brings me up with the tying run on third and one out.

My big moment, my chance to erase all doubts back in Philly that I'm a money player. Instead, I strike out, and I go in search of the nearest hole to crawl into. In that moment, walking from home to the dugout, I see my entire career flash before me. How can I live down this new failure? No matter what good I did in the past, I've failed in the moment of my team's greatest need. Their offensive leader and highest-paid player, I've blown my greatest opportunity ever to deliver in the clutch.

Del Unser lifts this burden before I get my bat in the rack with a pinch-hit single to right. Game tied! Then series MVP Manny Trillo triples over the third base bag, scoring both runners, and all hell breaks loose in our dugout. Ruthven shuts out the tired Astros easily in the bottom of the tenth.

We're going to the World Series!

I remember the joy I felt for our team, coupled with a feeling of acute personal disappointment. I guess there was no reason to be that hard on myself, other than that was my nature. Maybe that in itself was a good reason for discomfort in those situations. I didn't relish them the way Pete did. I was simply too afraid to fail, and that affected my ability to succeed under pressure.

The clubhouse celebration went on and on. Manny got his MVP award. Everyone got champagne showers. Finally, exhausted from the weekend, we boarded the team bus. For some reason, I was the last one to get on, and a round of applause greeted me. My teammates actually applauded. I can still see Greg Luzinski's smile in the first seat. They were saying, "Thanks for getting us here," and I never felt so close to a group of teammates in my life. They picked me up and carried me into the World Series.

"Now the fun starts," Pete told me as we flew home to meet the Royals, who had swept the Yankees. He told me to enjoy every minute of it. He said the World Series was icing on the cake, that the real pressure was in the playoffs. The atmosphere back home in the Vet was electric, with 65,000 people rocking the place. We won the first two games, and off we went to Kansas City.

(On a side note, remember George Brett's well-publicized hemorrhoids problem? Well, he wasn't the only third baseman in that Series to have them. Only mine weren't a matter of public knowledge; mine were serious.)

The games in Kansas City were a different story. Their bats came alive. They pounded us for two days. In game four, Larry Christienson got just one out, and Dickie Noles replaced him. Dickie was a gunslinger, the kind of guy you avoided eye contact with in a bar. Dickie decided to put an end to this Royals hitting party, so he waited for the right moment. And he got it.

Bottom of the fourth, George Brett comes up with one out and the bases empty. He eases into the first pitch with his front foot close to the plate and takes it. His house, his plate. (Hey, the guy hit .390 that year!) That's not the way Dickie sees it. Noles rockets the next pitch right over Brett's right ear, putting Brett flat on his back. As George is dusting himself off, Royals manager Jim Frey jumps out of the dugout and beelines for the mound, but Pete intercepts him before he gets to the foul line. After a little milling around, everybody calms down.

More important, KC's bats calmed down. After that pitch—I call it the greatest brushback in World Series history—the Royals batted under .200 the rest of the way. One pitch turned the 1980 World Series around. We went on to win game five when Unser doubled me in with nobody out in the top of the ninth to tie the game and scored the winner on an infield single by Trillo. We headed home needing one win to become World Champs.

Carlton gave us seven innings, McGraw gave us two, and I drove in the winning run with an early single. Taking the field for the final three outs was surreal. The clock read 11:11, to this day my lucky time. Policemen on horseback ringed the field. I looked at Tug and said, "Neighbor, let's count 'em down. We need three."

We got the first two, then McGraw ran a deep count on Willie Wilson and struck him out swinging to end the game and the Series. Immediately Tug looked toward third with his arms out waiting on me, the way we had planned on the way to the game that afternoon. The rest of the scene is captured in a photo that hangs on my office wall today, one that will never leave my home. It sums up the entire 1980 season, and, most of all, how my teammates carried me, as they did in the picture, when I needed it most.

Chris Wheeler, our media relations guy, came to get me on the field, told me I was the Series MVP, and that we had to run down to the press conference. We stood there, and stood there, but no conference, and finally went back to the clubhouse just in time to miss the trophy presentation and the beginning of the celebration.

This time, my timing was a little off.

The Philly media reacted typically over the next couple days, disagreeing with the choice of me for MVP, saying Boone, McBride, and Bowa were just as deserving. They sure were, and just as easily could have been, but did the media need to rain on my parade? I hit safely in every game, drove in seven runs, hit two home runs, and played every inning—and did it all with a bad case of hemor- rhoids!

The parade saluting us as World Champions carried the dream to a new level. A million fans lining Broad Street, dangling from lampposts, standing on cars, hanging out of windows, all paying tribute to their Phillies. The parade passed by the Vet and ended in old JFK Stadium, where Harry Kalas's golden voice expressed our appreciation to our fans. We felt their warmth. We were bonded together as one. Maybe we would never be booed again.

Hey, at times like that, you think some really crazy thoughts.

4 Turn Out the Lights

The Phillies were the 1980 World Champions, I was the unanimous National League MVP, we figured to be better in 1981, and we believed we had the makings of a dynasty.

At least that was the plan.

Personally, I was at the top of my game in 1981. I hit .316, ran away with most of the power categories, and was crowned MVP for the second straight year.

The Phillies front office, however, had begun to dismantle the 1980 team before the season with the sale of Greg Luzinski to the White Sox. That was a sad day for Phillies fans, who would see most of the team depart over the next couple of years. So much for our dynasty.

Then the season, which began under the cloud of yet another labor dispute, was shattered by a fifty-day strike. The season was divided into halves. We won the first half, the Expos won the second, and we played them in a mini-series for the NL East division title. Steve Rogers pitched a shutout to beat Steve Carlton and send us home. We were just as good in 1981 as we'd been in 1980, maybe better, but we watched the postseason on TV.

The dismantling escalated. In December 1981, Bob Boone was sent to the Angels. We traded Keith Moreland, Dickie Noles, and Dan Larson to the Cubs. In January 1982 we traded Bowa and a skinny kid named Ryne Sandberg to the Cubs. Bake McBride went to the Indians. And we traded five guys—Manny Trillo, George Vukovich, Jay Baller, Julio Franco, Jerry Willard—for a young outfielder named Von Hayes. (Hence Von's nickname, "Five-for-One.")

All this was a direct result of free agency. The Phillies traded guys who would soon become free agents rather than lose them for nothing. Manny Trillo, for example, wanted top dollar or he was going elsewhere, so we traded him. On the other hand, the organization signed Ed Farmer, the top reliever in the American League, as a free agent. This was new to us, as we had come into the 1980s as a homegrown team and hadn't been accustomed to many roster changes.

Welcome to the Age of Free Agency.

The 1983 team was built to win *now*, and that's exactly what we did. Before the season began, we acquired Tony Perez, so now we had Rose, Morgan, and Perez. They called us "Wheeze Kids." (Hey, I was an eleven-year vet pushing thirty-four.) Wheeze schmeeze: We won the NL East by six games.

Imagine, sharing a clubhouse with three of the greatest Reds of all time. Those guys were amazing to be around. They talked trash all day, every day, and had forgotten more about winning than most teams ever knew. But each was nearing the end and knew it.

Well, maybe not Pete; he was still chasing Ty Cobb.

Funny how things—some good, some not so good—stick with you. For instance, at home against Montreal on May 28, I struck out three times against Expos starter Charlie Lea and once against Ray Burris. Then, thank goodness, came rain. The odd thing wasn't the four Ks; I'd done that before, and would do it again. The odd thing is, and I guarantee it's unique in baseball history, those four Ks took only twelve pitches. Good morning, good afternoon, good night—in each at-bat. If I swung, I missed. If I took, it was a strike. I challenge anyone to strike out four times on twelve pitches. The game was close all the way, so the crowd was into it. They stood and cheered as I approached the plate, then stood and booed as I went back to the dugout.

Now, during the rain delay, which I hoped would last forever, I was shocked, embarrassed, mad as hell. I told Tony Perez I wanted to quit baseball, that this was as low as you could go, and he cheered me up as only Doggie could. In his broken English he said, "Fuck it, man. Shit happens. Maybe you'll win this thing." The rain stopped, and with the score tied and two out, I hit the thirteenth pitch I'd seen that night for a game-winning home run. I rounded the bases, took high fives from my teammates, walked into the clubhouse, grabbed my car keys, and drove home in my uniform.

Later that year, we squared off against Los Angeles in the NLCS. Carlton beat the Dodgers 1–0 in game one on my first-inning home run. We went home needing two of three, where Sarge Matthews, the series MVP, got the big hits and led us into the 1983 World Series. Redemption from 1977 and 1978 was sweet. So was my nice, quiet 7 for 15, which went largely unnoticed with Sarge leading the charge.

I wish my next twenty at-bats, the ones against the Orioles in the World Series, had gone equally unnoticed.

We opened in Baltimore on a rainy, dreary night. This should have been a walk in the park. With all due respect, the Orioles weren't as good as the Dodgers or a couple of other teams in our league. Except for Eddie Murray and Cal Ripken, they were short offensively. And their pitching, which ultimately proved the difference, didn't look all that intimidating.

Just shows why you play the games.

We split the first two games; I was 0–8. Next it was the Vet for three. We roughed up Mike Flanagan over four innings in game three, but their bullpen shut us down. We're down two games to one. I'm now 0–12. In game four, the Orioles bullpen once again stopped us in our tracks. I get a broken bat single: 1–16. Game five was a must-win for us. Instead, Scott McGregor walked through us with a complete game five-hitter. I got none of them to finish the Series 1 for 20. It was over.

It was also over for the Wheeze Kids. In October, Rose and Morgan were released. In December, Perez was sold to the Reds. Earlier, old friends Dick Ruthven, Bill Robinson, and Ed Farmer were either traded or released. The Phillies were obviously committed to going with the kids in 1984, when I would turn thirty-five years old.

We finished 81–81 in 1984, falling to third. I kept plugging away with 36 home runs and 106 RBI, both leading the league, but I was feeling my age—and the pain from nagging muscle pulls in my legs throughout the year. Another blow came in November when we released Tug McGraw.

Following the 1984 season, a good friend of mine, Alan Flashner, aware that I was on the decline physically, hooked me up with a local guy named Pat Croce, head of a company called Sports Physical Therapists Inc. Pat was a licensed therapist with a clinic in nearby Broomall, Pennsylvania. But he was also a black belt in karate, a triathlete, and an "I Feel Good!" psycho. He would eventually sell his operation for a boatload of bucks, become president of the Philadelphia 76ers, morph into a TV analyst, and host a national talk show. I always remind him that the day I walked into his clinic was the beginning of the rise of his empire.

Actually, he did more for me than I did for him. He was the Flyers strength and conditioning coach when I first met him, and in later years he would train the Sixers. Pat became my fitness guru and one of my closest friends. He basically rebuilt my body with cardiovascular and weight training, restored the flexibility in my legs, and established a workout routine that I'm still addicted to today.

In 1985, I moved to first base to make room for a scrappy prospect named Rick Schu. I loved it. At first, you're in on almost every play. You can talk trash with the opposing players, umps, and coaches. After a slow start, I rebounded to have a decent year, hitting .277 with 33 homers and 93 RBI. We finished 75–87, our first losing season since my rookie year in 1974.

(If the Rick Schu experiment had worked out, playing first might have extended my career. But the following season I returned to third, and the year after that Rick was traded to Baltimore.)

Oh, there was one other thing Philly fans remember about 1985: my wig.

Late in the season, on the way to another home loss, just about all the fans had gone home, except for four or five hundred idiots ganged up behind the dugout who were really wearing us out, cursing at us through several rain delays. Anyway, in the papers the next day, I was accurately quoted as having referred to them as a mob. Then on Sunday, from Montreal, in an interview with Tony Kubek on national TV before the Game of the Week, I repeated my assessment of the Philly fans that night.

We returned home on Monday for a series with the Cubs, and everyone knew I was in trouble. My teammates wouldn't stand near me in pregame drills; I think they were afraid of a sniper. Back in the clubhouse after BP, I walked by Larry Andersen's locker and saw this long, black wig. Larry kept us loose with pranks and costumes, and he was generally the instigator of all clubhouse fun. Just for a laugh, I put it on. Then Steve Jeltz gave me his Porsche sunglasses, and—*presto!*—I had a disguise. I could go on the field incognito.

(Yeah, sure, like I wasn't wound way too tight for a stunt like that.)

But the guys started ragging me, saying I had no guts, daring me to do it, saying the fans wouldn't know what to do if I went out in that getup. So, scared out of my mind, I went with it. The fans freaked out. They'd come for blood, at least some of them, and at first they seemed dumbfounded—and then they started to laugh and cheer. I guess it showed them I wanted to acknowledge the tongue-lashing I'd given them, and to show them a human side of me they'd never seen.

In the latter half of 1985, I made a hitting discovery that carried me through the end of my career: I learned to "swing down" on the ball—the way Albert Pujols and Gary Sheffield do so well today—and not try to lift it in the air. It happened against Dwight Gooden with a man on third and one out. I decided to force myself, no matter what or where the pitch, to drive it on the ground to get the run in. I got a high fastball, one I normally couldn't handle, and drove it off the scoreboard in right center for a two-run home run. From that at-bat through 1987, I hit close to .300. After fifteen seasons, I finally felt like a great hitter, a really tough out. A good hitter, not just a dangerous hitter.

There's a big difference.

This stroke played out in 1986, when I won my third MVP award at age thirty-seven. The Mets ran away with the NL East, winning by twenty-one games over us. Von Hayes had a fantastic year, hitting .305, with 107 runs and 98 RBI. Generally written off as an underachiever, Von was a victim of timing. Had he come along five years earlier and been surrounded by good players and good pitching, his entire career might have been different. No one loved Philly more and wanted to win more.

Keeping up with my off-season workout program, I hit 35 homers and drove in 113 runs in 1987. Glenn Wilson took over as my sidekick when Ed Farmer left. And Lance Parrish signed with us as a free agent during spring training. Lance was the strongest man I ever met in baseball. Glenn got me listening to WXTU (Philly's country station) and buying country tapes and wearing Wranglers. We lived to see Glenn do his impressions. (The best: Nolan Ryan's windup and delivery.) Then there were Bedrock and Dutch—Steve Bedrosian, Cy Young winner in 1987 and one of the funniest men I've ever known; and Darren Daulton, one of the greatest Phillies ever.

The best of times. Times you can only dream of having as a kid. The 1970s and 1980s were my time, my era, my generation. I can't imagine playing at any other time. For me, and I can't be expected to be impartial, I played in the best era in baseball history.

But, like everything else, it had to come to an end.

5 All Good Things

It started in 1988. Something every veteran ballplayer eventually experiences. The beginning of the end.

What used to be easy begins to become hard. Range in the field. Aggressiveness on the bases. And, most important, bat speed.

They fade away, right before your eyes. Nagging injuries take longer to heal. The travel, the autographing, the day-to-day responsibilities you used to take for granted become burdensome. You start thinking the unthinkable: life without baseball.

The thing that bothered me most, however, was losing.

For the Phillies, 1988 was a rebuilding year to forget, with new GM Lee Thomas at the controls. Lee came over from the Cardinals, where he'd been director of player development. Over the next two years, Lee cleaned house, bringing in new staff and, in 1989, former Cardinals third base coach Nick Leyva as manager.

My presence had to make it very tough for Lee to build the team he wanted. I was coming off two productive years, one of which, 1986, was my third MVP season, so he was forced to build around me—even though I was thirty-eight. I was closing in on the 550-home-run plateau (I entered the 1988 season with 530), and that, combined with our losing record and a budding youth movement, put the media's focus directly on my shoulders. That was okay; it was why I was getting paid the big bucks. But the losing was starting to wear me down.

In early summer, I developed a pain on the tip of my right shoulder. It hurt when I lifted my arm above shoulder level. It was a sharp pain that seemed to get worse the more I tried to hit with it. But I kept plugging away for over two months. I finally went on the DL on August 13, hoping therapy and rest would improve it. I traveled with the team, took my scheduled therapy and exercise, and watched from the dugout. A couple of days before my return, I took batting practice to test it out. Still weak and reluctant to turn it loose, I opted for more therapy time. It never healed.

In early September, I had a consultation with Phillies orthopedist Dr. Philip Marone and trainer Jeff Cooper. Marone's diagnosis was bleak. He said I needed major corrective surgery to repair a rotator cuff. To understand my problem better, imagine not being able to paint a wall with an up-and-down motion. Dr. Marone suggested that Donna and I go home and discuss the operation—and a possible future without baseball.

The MLBPA had negotiated, as part of the last Collective Bargaining Agreement, the right for a player to obtain a second opinion on injuries. So at Pat Croce's recommendation, I went to see Dr. James Andrews in Birmingham, Alabama. Dr. Andrews, with due respect to many other noted orthopedic surgeons, was then the top guy in the world, especially when it came to shoulders. A "celebrity wall" of photographs of patients in his office in 1988 included, among others, Jack Nicklaus and Roger Clemens.

(Can you believe it? Dr. Andrews operated on Roger Clemens's shoulder in 1985, and the Rocket's still going strong, leading the majors in 2005 with a 1.97 ERA.)

Dr. Andrews examined me and determined that he could go in

arthroscopically and correct my problem, but the rehab would be up to me. This sounded a hell of a lot better than slicing my shoulder open, so I returned soon thereafter for the procedure.

Shortly thereafter, with the help of a therapist, I moved my right arm through its full range. The postsurgery pain is indescribable. The traumatized area doesn't want to move right away, but because of the arthroscopic procedure, which did not require an incision, you can still move it. The six-month rehab, with the goal of returning to the Phillies, was my inspiration.

The kicker is I wasn't offered a contract for the 1989 season, so I became a free agent. Injured shoulder, rehab, Dr. Marone's original diagnosis, whatever—to the Phillies and twenty-five other "colluding" teams, I was damaged goods. Sure, I'd been injured, and I had surgery. But many players had similar surgery, recovered, and returned to form. Why shouldn't I?

Eventually, the Phillies and I agreed on a four-part incentive-based contract that would put me at $2 million should I attain all levels: (1) make the team, (2) remain on the team through June 1, (3) remain on the team through August 1, and (4) finish the season. It was like pulling teeth getting this deal, almost like they were betting against me.

Now, this was in the heart of the 1987–90 period, when the baseball owners were colluding to slow down player movement and increases in salary by agreeing not to offer free agents more money than the team that stood to lose them. This forced players to take the best offer from their former teams. I got one offer, from Pete and the Reds to come to Cincinnati: $1 million—less than my past salary. Did one single American League team approach me to be a designated hitter? No.

I worked my butt off the next six months, every day, lifting, stretching, lifting, stretching, and more lifting. In January, I started throwing from ten feet in the rehab clinic, then farther, then in the parking lot, and eventually in Florida on the field. On the way to spring training, I stopped to see Dr. Andrews and got my release to play. Medically, I was healed, but I was gun-shy about letting my arm go and turning my swing loose. The entire spring, I didn't come close to a home run. The press questioned whether I'd return 100 percent by Opening Day—or ever.

Some days the arm felt strong, others it felt cranky. Truthfully, I never regained my ability to throw the ball aggressively across the diamond from third. I tended to throw sidearm, a more comfortable slot, whenever I could. It was hard to throw overhand.

With a bat in my hands, I felt a little different. I always believed I could figure out a way to hit. After not hitting a home run all spring, I hit one on Opening Day off Greg Maddux, and all was well.

The early going was tough, though. I treated it as just another slow start, but I was a little late on fastballs that in past years I would have crushed. Every fly ball seemed to land on the warning track. Looking back, I think blaming everything on age or injuries was a convenient excuse. If we'd been a winning ball club, I would have sucked it up and found a way to contribute. If I'd been moved back to first base, I would have continued to play, but we had a young prospect named Ricky Jordan, who the Phillies were very high on, and they wanted him to play every day. Quite simply, my age, my physical condition, and the losing combined to wear me down.

Before our first game in Los Angeles, on what was to become my last road trip, I went to the stadium early as usual. I remember stepping on the scale and weighing 215 pounds, 10 over my normal playing weight, and deciding that committing to an in-season workout program before games would get my body and—more important—my mind back on the right track.

So I jumped into my shorts and headed to the field for a long run. After about half a lap of the field, something popped in my back, and I had to return to the trainer's room. I felt old and out of shape. I didn't think of retiring immediately, but the end was looming.

We lost two of three games against the Dodgers, and I had two hits, one a drop-bunt single, which would soon become significant. Next we went to San Francisco and got swept by the Giants. The season was already a grind, and it was only May.

I started to feel like I was getting in the way. I wasn't contributing, and although I knew manager Nick Leyva was in my corner, I also knew he had to be taking heat about keeping me in the four hole. The focus of the team during that period was basically me—and my home run total. This was uncomfortable, and the losing only made the situation worse. I started looking for real signs, and I also prayed for direction, as this was a life decision that would affect a lot of people. My hitting slump continued. I went 2 for 21 on the road trip, which along with the losing was a sign in itself.

Then, during the Sunday getaway game, came the epiphany. The Giants had men on first and second, and Robby Thompson hit a double-play ground ball right at me. It went through my legs and into left to load the bases. Another sign, this one that I was losing it defensively. It was almost like I didn't want to be in the game, like I was afraid of the ball. In my prime, I would have taken a broken nose rather than let that ball go through me.

The final sign came on the next pitch, a Will Clark grand slam. As he rounded the bases and ran in front of me at third base, I made my decision: This was my last game.

Just recalling it puts a lump in my throat.

I dreaded the announcement, the press conference, the cameras in my face, the interviews, a media circus, all that would go with it, but at the same time, and most of all, I felt relief. It was time. The weight would be off my shoulders. I saw a Phillies team free to rebuild, to move on without me as the ball and chain.

Now I had to finish the game knowing all this and stay bound to my decision. In what I thought was my last at-bat, I hit a slow roller to short, a tough play for Jose Uribe, and beat it out for a single. A small rally in the ninth allowed me to hit again off Mike LaCoss, and I walked. On first base, I said to Tony Taylor, our coach, "TT, that was my last at-bat." I don't think he believed me.

So, my last "official" at-bat was an infield single—until a scoring change after the game turned it to an error. I don't know what to read into that one, but how odd—a slow roller to short, a tough play, a single, and it's changed to an error. Maybe I should have complained, but I had another issue on my mind: retiring. That made my last base hit that bunt single way back in L.A.

My first hit in my first full year in the majors, 1973, was also a bunt single. Bookend bunt singles, sixteen years apart, with 548 homers stacked in the middle.

The next hour was a blur. I showered, tipped the clubhouse man, gathered my bags, and headed outside to the bus. The trip to the airport took forever. This was the period of truth, the time when the solace of silence and reflection was going to test my decision. We were going to San Diego, my favorite road town, and I knew a new environment could change things. I also knew the strength of my decision in San Francisco. If I changed my mind, then every time the rest of the year that things went bad on the field, I'd want to walk. Not a good way to approach the game.

So I stuck to my guns, and as the team was boarding the plane, I asked Nick Leyva to join me on the tarmac. I told Nick I had decided to retire. He knew I had been going through some rough times, physically and mentally, and he knew our team was going nowhere. He tried to change my mind, but we both knew deep down that it was time. He asked, "Have you thought this over?" I said yes, I had. My retirement was official. Nick said thanks for everything, and told me he would inform Mr. Giles and Lee Thomas of my decision.

The next twenty-four hours were the most emotional of my professional life. As my teammates slowly got the news, an impromptu party, led by Bedrock and Dutch, began to take life. We never had a problem pulling something like that together on short notice. It became my private team farewell party, and I'll never forget it. As the players filtered in, each of them hugged me and shared a private thought related to our friendship. My closest friends—veterans like Daulton, Bedrosian, Hayes, and Chris James—shared tears with me. There's no stronger emotional bond than to have another man hug you and tell you he loves you. My final hours as a ballplayer were among the most intense, most memorable times of my life.

I called Donna and my parents. Donna was very supportive and very emotional, but sensed it was best for me. Now I'd be home with her and the kids. We had devoted our entire marriage to my career, and now life could be about family, not baseball. We had a whole new life ahead of us.

The news triggered many more wonderful hugs and thanks from men I'd traveled with over the eighteen years, guys like Harry Kalas, Richie Ashburn, and Chris Wheeler. I had scripted a small farewell speech for the press conference, one I now see was pretty pathetic. The opening line, "Twenty years ago I left Dayton, Ohio, with two bad knees . . ." Well, it just flat stunk.

What I was trying to say was that when I departed from home twenty years ago, the odds of me standing before a national TV audience explaining why I couldn't play another game—I was done at 2,404—were off the charts. I had no chance of doing what I did, but it happened.

Most retirement press conference speeches are similar. If your stature requires major coverage, then you spent most of the previous twenty years or so giving your life to the game. People do this in all walks of life. In sports, though, the pressure, preparation, commitment, and joy of teamwork, while you are playing at a level that only a very small percentage of people have ever played, become extra special. Leaving the "life," the only one I'd known for twenty-five years, was a daunting task.

I made my official announcement on TV, spoke to the media, did a couple of one-on-one interviews, had a visit from the Padres players (which was especially nice), and headed back to the hotel to pack. I couldn't stay around. I needed to end it. The next stop was home. One more press conference with the local and regional media, and then it would be over. Donna met me at the airport in Philadelphia, and a limo whisked us off to the Vet. Once again, I made a small speech at home plate to the local media, Phillies employees, and whoever else was interested. Bill Giles and I shed some serious tears of joy, having understood each other's role in the overall scheme of my career. There would be other celebrations to come, but I never had to worry about the pressure of performing on the field again.

It was over.

I say that with mixed feelings, as I always wished that I could have enjoyed being Mike Schmidt more than I did. I never really allowed myself to have fun on the field. Actually, the real joy started then, when I began to see who I was, finally understand what I meant to my teammates, the Phillies organization, and my fans. The blinders were removed. For the first time, I could see and feel everyone around me.

If only I could have had that experience while in uniform . . .

Well, I can't do it over. But I learned from my mistakes. And I'll always be comforted by the knowledge that I couldn't have given one more ounce of myself on the field to the game of baseball, the game we all love.

Suddenly, after two decades, I was out of baseball. But was baseball out of me? I thought it was, at least for a while. But when I returned to the game—this time the way I began, as a fan—I found that baseball had changed.

And I was confused by what I was seeing.

6 The Worst of Times

After the dust cleared following my retirement in 1989, I was faced with a scary decision: what to do with the rest of my life. Being retired at the age of forty might sound appealing to some people, but the prospect of finding new goals and interests to keep me active was challenging.

The remainder of the 1989 season was easy enough to handle. We traveled with the kids, enjoyed being normal, and didn't miss baseball in any way, shape, or form. That might be a little strong. Sure, I tuned in to the games now and then to watch my old buddies, and I watched a few innings of the postseason. But to say I was a fan would be a stretch. Over the next couple of years, though busy enough, I was a bit lost. Slowly but surely, I needed to feel "needed" again, especially by those who ran the game. I knew little, to this point in my life, about something I'd need to get used to: rejection.

As much as I wanted to think I was missed around the Phillies, the truth is that there was a sense of relief among people in the organization that I was no longer part of the equation. The "Schmidt cloud" had been lifted. Lee Thomas now had the freedom to shuffle the roster without me. He acted immediately by getting Lenny Dykstra and John Kruk, who breathed new life into the team. New uniforms were designed. Dykstra, Kruk, and Daulton became the new Philly household names. They caught on big time with their long hair, baggy uniforms, and carefree style. And they were for real, beating Atlanta and going to the World Series in 1993. Like my team a decade earlier, their run ended in a World Series loss, this time to Toronto, but the "wild bunch" left their mark.

My initial plans were set in my mind, and ready to be put in motion. With all my solid relationships and friends in the front office, especially owner Bill Giles, I believed I'd have no trouble finding a role as soon as I made it known I was ready. Perhaps manager someday. Or—like Brett, Ryan, or Reggie—a position as assistant to the president. Bill had confided in me privately many times over my career, and so why wouldn't we make a good team now? There had to be a place for me in management. There's no way so many people could respect you so much as a player, and seemingly as a person, and not see value in you as a member of their executive management team.

Not even close. Not even a coaching job. Pretty quickly I sensed they'd just as soon see me move on. I must have read the whole thing wrong. It's human nature, I guess. If I worked for the Yankees, the last guy I'd want managing my team, or working in the office next to me, would be Reggie Jackson. All the focus would be on him, the way it had been when he was playing. What does a guy like that know about managing or running an organization?

And there's another thing: I sometimes spoke my piece too bluntly, without first thinking through the possible repercussions. Two times, in particular, come to mind.

The first was in 1986 when I told a reporter that the dugouts and runways at the Vet had come to smell like . . . Wait a minute. Maybe I'd better tell the whole story.

I was at a luncheon celebrating the release of my *Road to 500* video, an event attended by representatives of the Philadelphia sports media. Following the speeches, Stan Hochman, a writer for the *Philadelphia Daily News*, cornered me, and we got into a general discussion about the Phillies organization, past and present. I told Sam I thought the organization wasn't as attentive to details as it once had been, and that certain things—the AstroTurf, the dugouts, the clubhouses—weren't being maintained as immaculately as in the past. I told Stan that we actually had a family of stray cats roaming under the stands after hours, and that the dugout runway to the clubhouse smelled like cat piss.

Needless to say, I said this without thinking, as I should have, that he was taking it all down, and certainly without meaning to disrespect the people responsible for stadium maintenance. The next day, Stan's *Daily News* article reported—accurately, I'm afraid—what I had said. That afternoon when I arrived at the clubhouse, I found a sweeper, disinfectant, and other household cleaning articles in my locker, plus a bouquet of flowers. The worst part, of course, was that I had unintentionally offended several close friends, especially clubhouse man Kenny Bush and stadium operations director Mike DeMuzio. I should have been smart enough to know that (a) the stadium was managed by the City of Philadelphia, and (b) certain friends might be hurt by seeing my words in print.

I drove another nail into my coffin when I was quoted in a Philadelphia publication following my retirement as saying, "The Phillies are my team." I meant simply that I had given my life to the Phillies—which I had. To this day, I cannot understand how anybody could think otherwise. But some in the front office evidently did.

(P.S.: The dugout runway *did* smell like cat piss.)

• • •

Perception and reality often diverge, and I believe they did with regard to me. As my status in the game grew, the general perception of me changed. Deep down, no matter whom I passed in home runs or what honor I received, I was still the same insecure guy who just wanted to be part of the team. But I think I was perceived as a person who thought he was bigger than the team, who always needed special treatment, who could not blend in. Yes, I was granted some special treatment—sometimes needed, always appreciated—but I didn't consider *myself* special. After I retired, I wanted to join the Phillies management team, but the perception of me prevented it.

I became a dilemma for the Phillies. On special occasions, they needed me to be Mike Schmidt for drawing power, but they were afraid of Mike Schmidt as a member of management.

I guess I can understand. I genuinely try to. Where would I have fit in? Where would my presence and my opinion not have been the focus of disproportionate public attention? And, with my history of frankness with the press, how could I have been counted on to be diplomatic? Strange, ten or fifteen years ago, those questions might have had some validity. But now?

In 1990, with the Phillies management door not even ajar, I took the normal path to staying in contact with the game: broadcasting. The Phillies' cable partner at that time was a company called Prism. I became a member of the Prism Phillies broadcast team, which included Garry Maddox, Chris Wheeler, and Jim Barniak. My assignment schedule was for around twenty-five home games, just enough to stay connected.

I enjoyed the broadcast, but I wasn't a good fit. For the most part, my natural speaking voice was too soft and my personality too low-key for TV. I had to be constantly reminded to speak up and put more energy into my voice. I just couldn't fake excitement when a guy singled up the middle, and I got tired of the standard comments like "I spoke to him before the game" or "That was a good piece of hitting" that are so common in broadcasts today. I couldn't get comfortable hanging around the clubhouses in my blazer trolling for a sound bite, or in the booth overreacting to what was taking place on the field.

Though I felt I had a knack for interesting insights and observations, I couldn't complete them in five seconds. God forbid you should talk over a pitch, any pitch, in any situation. I couldn't bring myself to see that a ball, low and away, on a 1–1 count with the bases empty in a lopsided game, was automatically more important than some point I was trying to make about a certain team or player.

I did do the 1989 NLCS as cohost of the pregame show with Marv Albert, and I worked the dugout during the games. (My mom said I was damn good, I might add.) After CBS acquired the broadcast rights to Major League Baseball in 1989, I entered my name as a possible analyst for the CBS Game of the Week. I went to New York to interview with Neil Pilson, head of CBS Sports, but he and his people chose Tim McCarver and Jim Kaat.

Rejection and more rejection—a new, real-world element I had to learn to deal with. My response was understandable but unproductive: I lost interest in the Phillies and baseball in general. I was always willing to accommodate them on promotional game nights, and I've always been treated warmly by the organization when I've done so—and by the fans. But frankly, I began to feel the guy in me who played baseball for twenty years was a totally different person, not the same fellow who was being rejected in his search for a smooth place to land.

It seemed clear to me that I was ready to move on, without baseball. And it seemed clear that baseball was ready to move on without me.

• • •

But just as I thought baseball and I had parted ways, a really cool opportunity came along in 1992: I was asked to be a part of an owner- ship group pursuing the newly awarded expansion franchise in South Florida. This would mean going from a broken-down, some- what bitter old ballplayer to part owner of a brand-new big league ballclub at the age of forty-two.

It took me about ten seconds to say yes.

For almost a year, I traveled back and forth from Philadelphia to South Florida, meeting and greeting politicians and community leaders, and helping develop our group's formal presentation to Major League Baseball's expansion committee. I visited Joe Robbie Stadium in Miami with our group to offer my opinion on the pro- posed baseball layout and tour the location of our future offices.

It was exhilarating, because it represented a whole new page in my life. I was getting a small ownership piece, and I was going to be GM of our new ballclub. I was back, baby! No more worries about what I was going to do with the rest of my professional life. I'd use every ounce of energy, just like when I played, only this time to build a club from scratch. Heck, we'd go beat the Phillies! There was no downside. I already wanted to move to Florida in the worst way. Now I had a perfect reason. Bring on the coat and tie!

You see, I thought we were a lock. There were three groups competing for the right to pay the $135 million for the franchise, but our group—organized by Rick Horrow and headed financially by entrepreneur Morton Davis—was rock solid. We had it all. Donna and I went shopping for a home in Fort Lauderdale.

I remember the appearance before the expansion committee in New York during interview week. It was a Monday morning, and we were the first group up. In my presentation, I explained my player development philosophy and several other elements related to my job. The other members of our group each spoke for five minutes.

Our presentation was a perfect 10—we couldn't have done better. We had deep, Miami-based pockets; influential partners; the support of state and local political leaders; and a future Hall of Famer as part owner and GM. How could we miss?

On our way out, I was introduced to the man who headed one of the other two ownership groups, a fellow by the name of Wayne Huizenga. He wasn't a baseball guy, but one member of his group was Carl Barger, the former president of the Pirates. That had to help, but later we found out that Blockbuster Video, one of Huizenga's recent acquisitions, had just become a licensee of Major League Baseball. Not bad timing, I'd say. I thought I was the guy with good timing. But not, so far, in business.

Six years later, the Florida Marlins—make that Wayne Huizenga's Florida Marlins—were the World Champions. Two years later, Huizenga dismantled his team. And a year after that, he sold the Marlins for $150 million and got out of baseball altogether.

Funny, sometimes the ball really does take some funny bounces.

My next target in this quest to find my future was in the sports agency business. Rick Horrow, who had headed the baseball ownership group, became the developer and head of Golden Bear International, a new sports management division of Jack Nicklaus's Golden Bear Inc. My job was to acquire clients from college and pro baseball. I visited and began discussions with Jason Giambi, Charles Johnson, Johnny Damon, Calvin Murray, and Jeffrey Hammonds, among others. The business was slow to start, and we were competing with established mega-buck agencies. Then the economy took a nasty dive, and at the end of a year, the project was put on hold.

Think I'm not cut out for TV? Try picturing me standing outside locker room doors waiting on clients.

For the better part of my twenty years of professional baseball, I was labeled as a player who "over thought" everything. I was called cocky . . . aloof . . . introspective . . . introverted . . . even, by some of the media guys, Mr. Cool. "If Schmitty would only stop thinking so much," people close to the team often said, "he might actually enjoy the game."

There's a lot of truth to that. My obsessive-compulsive-impulsive nature might have held me back: I really didn't enjoy the game as much as most other players. I made too much out of all the issues that confronted me, from the o-fers to the smell in the dugout.

My good friend and teammate, the late Tug McGraw, had it wired. He was a perfect fit for baseball. A free spirit who lived every day for what it presented, Tug loved the attention, and he let fans into his life. Basically, the exact opposite of me. He'll never know how much I wanted to be like him around the game.

Seems I always wanted to be something other than what I was. I think it's called insecurity. If anyone should have been secure, I should have been. After all, I had a long, successful career that took me to the Hall of Fame. But I wasn't what I projected on the outside—a cool, cocky guy who was in control, who accepted the spotlight, and who was happy to bear the responsibilities of stardom.

Not so. Not nearly so. Inside the clubhouse, I was comfortable with leadership; on the field, I preferred blending in. I played a "quiet" game. Intense and super-competitive, but quiet. I played with blinders on, like a racehorse, without looking to the right or left. I tried to lead the league in everything *and* stay under the radar at the same time. That's hard to do, but I knew it was the best fit for my personality, even though it isolated me from fans.

I wish I could have had the whole package—like, say, Reggie Jackson. Reggie thrived on being the star attraction. He wasn't afraid to bring attention to himself following a home run, or play to the crowd during a game. He was hated in visiting parks; I was cheered in visiting parks. The only place I occasionally felt hated was in Philadelphia during a bad slump.

I *did* think too much. Still do.

As an ex-ballplayer and lifelong student of the game, I plan. I study. I enjoy analyzing why things happen, how they happen, and why people do what they do.

As a player, I enjoyed the mechanical process of working out of a slump more than the results. I enjoyed the pregame preparation each day more than the game. When I was on my game, no one was ever better. When I started to leak a little oil, no one was quicker to look for change. "Hey, be patient," somebody would say. "You'll come out if it." My response was always the same: "I need to adjust *now*."

Good, bad, who knows? I had my critics, but I'm in the Hall of Fame, and most people say I was the greatest ever at my position. Not bad for an insecure psycho.

Physically, I probably could have played a couple more seasons. Mentally, my tank was empty. There wasn't another drop of brain matter left for baseball. Maybe that's the way it should be. I put it in the Lord's hands, and He flashed the sign. It was, "Move on, there's a whole new world out there for you." So, I'm content with my career and my decision to retire when I did.

I'm also content with my post-career life, despite the rejection I had to deal with in the early 1990s. It was tough, but I'm stronger for it. I'm still plugging away, setting lofty goals, moving from project to project, but now with the security and comfort of knowing exactly who I am.

Like me, baseball in the late 1990s got new life breathed into it. New fan-friendly ballparks were opening. Fans were returning. TV ratings were up. Thanks mainly to Mark McGwire, Sammy Sosa, and Barry Bonds, baseball seemed to be regaining its place in American consciousness. It felt like a fairy tale unfolding, and baseball would surely live happily ever after.

Unfortunately, behind the scenes something was brewing that would stop baseball in its tracks and cast a dark cloud over its future.

7 Looking for an Edge

My son played baseball in high school. He was a pitcher, but he also played the infield and the outfield, because his team had only twelve players most of the time. But Jonathan played a different game than I did. He played simply for the fun of it, the fun of being with his friends. He wanted to win and to become a better player, but never at the expense of fun. I couldn't understand it. I first thought, How ridiculous, you can't become the best with that attitude. Don't you *need* to be number one, to have winning be your first priority? That's the way I felt then. Now I look back and see it as refreshing and comforting to know that the game I devoted the first twenty years of my adult life to can actually be played for fun.

From the time I was a kid, through this morning when I woke up, I've wanted—no, *needed*—to be number one. I'm hard-wired to want to be the best, to win, and to think anything less is not worth pursuing. Oh, sure, I loved to play ball, but I needed to be the best, needed to win all my battles. That's how I was programmed and that's how all major league players are programmed. If they weren't driven in that way, they wouldn't be there. Once there, it only gets worse. I won the National League home run title eight times. Who the hell finished second? Other than his agent, who cares?

We are a society that looks at results, not effort. We look at wins and losses, not how the game was played. We grade on numbers, not sweat. And in our team sports, individual players are financially rewarded on their individual success, not their team's. That's kind of funny, if you think about it. Take a team and give each member $5 million if they win, and nothing if they lose, and watch how quick they start thinking "we."

Our society loves a winner, hates a loser. We want to be associated with winners. Why is attendance up when we are winning, and down when we are losing? Why do people get along in a winning environment, and not in a losing one? Why is a manager not a good leader when his team is losing?

Players are compared in order to establish their value. Player A hits 50 home runs per year and makes $15 million. Player B looks at Player A and wonders if Player A has an edge, something—maybe big, maybe little—that Player B doesn't have, but might get. A certain bat, a special training drill, a particularly knowledgeable coach, a potent dietary supplement . . . or maybe a performance-enhancing drug?

As long as society rewards people for winning, for being better than the competition, rather than on sweat and effort, much less on some intangible relating to the greater good of humanity, then competitors will look for every edge they can. And they're all going to agree on one thing: The playing field had better damn well be level.

But we now know that in baseball for a fifteen-year period, it wasn't.

Today's baseball players and their fans grew up in an ESPN world. They perform for fans who want the game to be an endless highlights reel. Average fans want more home runs, higher-scoring games, and nonstop action—and want it now. If they don't get it from a live baseball game, they can click to their Xbox or PlayStation and create it. They're used to getting what they want with the push of a button. They enjoy a pitchers' duel about as much as a public reading of the telephone book.

Part of the daily pressure in baseball comes not from playing the game but from living the life. That wasn't so difficult forty years ago, or even twenty. Now, cameras are everywhere, looking to catch everything a player does, particularly something that might be titillating or embarrassing or controversial. The media—print and electronic— hunt in packs, always ready to pounce on the slightest misstep or careless word. Autograph seekers stalk the players from hotel lobby to parking lot to clubhouse door. Hoping to grab a valuable signature that'll end up on eBay the following day, they hound players without any self-awareness of being intrusive or crossing the line. The only real privacy players have away from home or hotel room is in the clubhouse, where they spend far more time than my generation did.

But the number one source of pressure, the bottom-line reason that players are constantly on the lookout for an edge, is . . . the bottom line. As in money. As in $10 million a year for six years, guaranteed. As in one big season at the right time can set you and your family up for life—and one bad season at the wrong time can get you Designated for Assignment.

The money is mind-boggling. From A-Rod (averaging $25 million a year through 2009) to the major league minimum ($300,000), the salaries in baseball today are so huge that a player would be nuts if he didn't try to gain every possible edge. But the window of opportunity doesn't stay open for long: Your typical ballplayer's hanging up his spikes long before most people hit their peak earning years. And a ballplayer is always just one twisted knee or torn rotator cuff away from retiring before he turns thirty.

Look for every possible edge? You have to.

Look, if I had played in the 1990s, I would have considered using steroids. The temptation would have been tremendous because the stakes are so high. I sought out every edge I could get in the 1970s and 1980s, when steroids weren't around. Why wouldn't I be just as driven in the 1990s, when they were? If the right guy, at the right time, with the right formula for me showed up, why should I think I would have had the willpower to say no?

The right formula of anabolic steroids allows muscle groups to recover faster after exertion. This means you can lift more with the same amount of effort. Normal weight training regimen, twice the results. More body mass, more strength, and more confidence add up to a more intimidating presence at the plate. Sure, you still have to work out, you still have to have good mechanics, and you still have to hit the ball. But knowing that a controlled, contact swing will produce long home runs is a huge advantage.

Baseball is loaded with cheaters—or does it sound more polite to say "with crafty veterans looking for an edge"? We knew who threw a Vaseline ball, who scratched the ball with a tough finger-nail, and who used a tack in his glove. The Hall of Fame is full of pitchers who messed with the ball: Gaylord Perry's certainly not the Lone Ranger on that front. One year I wore golf spikes to get better traction on artificial turf.

Cheating? More like "edging."

Never has so much been at stake for baseball players. The money that comes with baseball success today is staggering. Our society is enamored with status obtained through money; you can achieve that status in baseball with one big contract. You can be featured on *ESPN Hollywood* if you're rich and famous. But what about the young player hoping to make it for the first time? Or the veteran journeyman trying to hang on? Or the fringe player whose batting average is dangerously close to the Mendoza Line?

What about the guy who sees the difference in earning the big league minimum and living the big league life being a little needle in the butt?

This is probably the guy with the most pressure, the guy who most likely took the fall before 2004. We'll never know. Most players who used steroids in the last fifteen years got away with it. Many are on big league teams right now, earning seven figures a year. They found their edge.

Random, unannounced testing for illegal performance-enhancing drugs will, I am convinced, clean up the game. The fear of testing positive and having a reputation shattered will keep most—maybe all—players straight. But it will be a slow process, and perhaps even some high-profile players could still test positive even though they've stopped using steroids.

Because of testing, today's players may soon come to fear anything stronger than Flintstones vitamins. They'll start reading labels on protein supplements and analgesic lotions as if they were guides to buried treasure. They'll boost their weight training, but not by opening a plastic bottle—at least until someone out there brews up a remedy that enables players to beat the testing procedure. There's always something just around the corner, especially if you have money to pay for it.

I know about looking for an edge. I spent my entire career on that quest. Who knows where that might have led me had a quick fix been available? But there wasn't, so I got my edge by working harder than anybody else. That was my security. Few players in my era prepared and practiced with my intensity. I was so driven to be the best player that I actually deprived myself of enjoying my success. I was obsessed with preparation. I was convinced that if I dedicated more time, focus, and sheer hard work to the game than my opponents did, I would eventually end up on top.

And I did.

But I'm not sure it was the right way. My son, Jonathan, would surely have had more fun.

Fun. I wonder what that would have been like?

8 Finding the Abyss

Suddenly baseball players were getting bigger—much bigger—right before our eyes. Huge tattooed biceps, rippling forearms, bulging necks, even pumped-up faces. Players who ended a season at 180 reported the following spring training at 210. Weight lifting? Sure, everybody was lifting weights by the early 1990s. Dietary supplements? Sure, protein shakes had become the clubhouse beverage of preference. Was the combination of weight lifting and dietary supplements enough to account for the physical transformation?

I doubt it.

Steroid use was the worst-kept secret in baseball for the better part of a decade. Actually, it wasn't any kind of a secret. Anybody who spent any time in a major league clubhouse knew that a lot of guys were juicing. There were so many dead giveaways: the swollen faces, the acne across the backs, and the new muscle mass that appeared overnight. Players were proud of their new bodies, and flaunted the look.

It was the times.

Everybody suspected it or knew about it, but nobody talked about it publicly. Some kept silent because they figured it was nobody else's business. Some did so probably because they were weighing the pluses and minuses of trying it themselves. And some, including everybody in the upper echelons of baseball's power structure—the Commissioner's Office and the Major League Baseball Players Association—turned a blind eye to the signs and the whispers because they didn't want to rock the boat.

After all, baseball was booming again. Big Mac and Sammy had saved baseball. The strike of 1994 was ancient history. Why mess with a good thing?

The little bottle of androstenedione discovered by a reporter in Mark McGwire's locker in 1998 sent up a red flag, but not very far up, and not many people paid much attention to it. I had for years been watching my teenage son consume shakes made with protein powder, so I didn't give McGwire's andro-whatever-it-was a second thought. Besides, I'd never heard of the stuff, and easily accepted Mark's explanation that he took it to help him recover faster from the aches and pains of playing ball, and from the grueling weight-training program he'd become famous for.

My take on it? Who cares? Who's pitching tomorrow?

The Commissioner of Baseball seemed equally unconcerned. Andro was on the banned list in the NFL, the NCAA, and the Olympics because of its chemical closeness to steroids that are on the Federal Government's banned substance list. But this was 1998, Mark McGwire was a national hero, and so the red flag was quickly lowered.

I first saw the effects of steroids in person in 1993 in an early season visit to the Phillies clubhouse. One Phillies player had gained 30 pounds over the off-season and was very proud of his new body. He'd also gone from a decent slap hitter to a five-tool player virtually overnight. More power to him, I figured. I shrugged it off as an isolated incident. He'd always been a little "out there" anyway. And who was going to complain about the sudden elevation in his overall game?

Turns out there were numerous guys like him around the league, guys who were either naive about the dangers or simply willing to put their health at risk over steroids—or, more likely, just plain ignorant of the potential dangers of what they were doing. (They weren't alone. At the time, I didn't even know that what was beginning to be called "juice" was illegal.) The game and its pressures will make you do funny things; sometimes all that matters to players is *now*.

Top athletes feel invincible. Their physical abilities set them apart from 99 percent of the rest of the world, so they figure their bodies can be pushed to the edge—and then some. Particularly in the early stages of their careers, they're young, they're resilient, and they're in top shape. Invincible? Try indestructible. I know, because I felt the same way as a player. The game, the life, livin' large, as we glorify it on TV today. I can't tell you how many nights I drove home from a game with four beers in me and another two in a bag on the seat. Many nights I'd get home and not even remember the drive. Invincible? Indestructible? Bull. Truth be known, I was lucky. Any one of those nights, one slip-up and my entire life would have been ruined.

I felt fan and peer pressure probably more than anyone could imagine, and I was vulnerable to about anything that came down the pike if it held out the promise, even the suggestion, of giving my game a boost. But I'm not so sure I'd have jumped if someone had offered me something that would add thirty pounds of muscle mass to my body. Back in the 1970s and early 1980s, only weight lifters, wrestlers, and football players craved more muscle mass. Arnold Schwarzenegger couldn't hit a major league fastball if his political career depended on it. Why would a baseball player want more muscle mass? Weight lifting by baseball players was actually frowned on back then. We feared losing flexibility in the upper body, leading to slow reactions at the plate. My generation never got a chance at steroids. We were lucky.

But we surely weren't squeaky clean. We had our tricks, and our vices, like every generation before and since. Don't think for a minute that the use of performance-enhancement chemicals started the day before yesterday. And don't think they're ever going to disappear until strict, Olympics-caliber testing procedures are instituted.

In my day, amphetamines—basically diet pills, commonly known as "greenies"—were widely available in major league clubhouses. They were obtainable with a prescription, but be under no illusion that the name on the bottle always coincided with the name of the player taking them before game time. Over-the-counter stimulants like NoDoz and Up Time also did the trick. Just ask a college student cramming for a midterm.

Look, most of us drink coffee on a daily basis, and most of us can feel the effects of caffeine as a mild stimulant. Ever hear somebody say, "I can't get going today without my two cups of coffee"? Sure you have. So what about a baseball player saying to himself, "I can't get going this morning—day game after a night game, two hours' sleep, facing Nolan Ryan (who slept eight hours) in front of 40,000 people—without a little help"?

Sure, we'd all like to believe this never occurs in our beloved game, but it does. These guys are human. No matter how much they're paid to play every day, some days you just don't have it. No, amphetamines and coffee are not the same thing. Yes, amphetamines are highly dangerous when abused. But the hard fact is that they have been around the game forever, and somewhere in some secret laboratory, the undetectable stimulant of the future is being concocted as you read these words.

Unlike the old days, when some of this stuff came out of the team trainer's bag, trainers and medical staff today do their best to police clubhouses and control what's available to players. I assure you, trainers today have absolutely nothing to do with any performance-enhancing drugs. But players conveniently ignore the guys they otherwise trust with their bodies, because these little helpers definitely contain an implied promise of "feeling good." And isn't "feeling good"—or at least forgetting that you feel bad—likely to enhance performance? In fact, what's enhanced is a player's sense of self-confidence in his performance, a sense that he has an edge he might not otherwise have.

Steroid use without medical supervision is illegal and dangerous. The ballplayer who obtained and used steroids without a prescription was breaking the law. He was also risking serious long-term damage to his health. But he convinced himself, with plenty of help from assorted "advisers," that the health issue was manageable and the risk was worth taking because of the big payoff: more power, more home runs—and more money. (Or, if he was a pitcher, more arm strength, more resilience—and more money.) Looking around, he saw a lot of other guys doing it. And he knew he could get away with it, because baseball didn't have a testing program, or even a rule against steroid use in the first place.

So he juiced.

Why? To gain that edge.

The red flag went up to stay on March 17, 2005, when a committee of the United States Congress stepped to the plate to take some cuts in a one-day hearing on the use of steroids in baseball.

Now, testing for steroids had been added to the Collective Bargaining Agreement back in 2002, but the associated penalties for testing positive didn't even add up to a slap on the hand. All players were to be tested anonymously for steroids in 2003. If a player tested positive, he would be required to undergo counseling, but his name would not be revealed. If a player tested positive *twice*, he would be publicly identified and either fined or suspended, at the discretion of the Commissioner of Baseball.

Then, in January 2005, as rumors of steroid use reached a crescendo, the MLBPA agreed for the first time to reopen the CBA in order to strengthen testing and penalties for steroid use. The result: first positive test—ten-day suspension; second—thirty days; third—sixty days; fourth—one year; fifth—penalty at the Commissioner's discretion.

More than a slap on the hand? Yes.

But enough? Congress—and a lot of people who love baseball—didn't think so.

As congressional investigations go, the March 17 hearing was pretty mild: no indictments, not much depth to the interrogation, and no serious follow-up. But it played out like the real deal, complete with star players, MLBPA leaders, and the Commissioner of Baseball, all with their right hands raised, all swearing to tell "the truth, the whole truth, and nothing but the truth . . . "

Problem is, some of them didn't.

Three current stars—Sammy Sosa, Rafael Palmeiro, Curt Schilling—were present, along with one retired megastar, Mark McGwire. Absent but present in spirit were three tainted stars—Barry Bonds, Jason Giambi, and Gary Sheffield—who had given testimony the year before to a San Francisco grand jury investigating the Bay Area Laboratory Company (BALCO), ground zero for the steroid movement on the West Coast.

Also present was Jose Canseco, because of the publication the preceding month of his tell-all book based on his own life and times: *Juiced: Wild Times, Rampant 'Roids, Smash Hits, and How Baseball Got Big.*

The hearing commenced with opening statements under oath by the commissioner, the three current players, and McGwire, in which each disavowed Canseco's allegations of rampant steroid use in major league baseball. But the principal focus swiftly fell on Mc-Gwire, who slammed Canseco's book but stopped short of denying he had ever used steroids. Way short. "I'm not here to talk about the past," McGwire said, over and over, except when he would shorten his response to "I'm retired."

In effect, Mark McGwire pleaded the Fifth Amendment.

"I don't have much to tell you," Sosa testified, after saying he had never used steroids, and nobody on the committee pressed him to.

"I have never used steroids," said Palmeiro, driving his message home with a stern look and a pointed finger. "Never. Period."

Schilling—an acknowledged king of communication—couldn't quite make clear exactly what, if anything, in his nineteen years of professional baseball, he'd seen or heard about steroids. He just knew those dudes at the plate with lumber in their hands were bigger than they used to be.

Canseco stood by the charges he made in his book.

McGwire's testimony was painful. The month before, responding to Canseco's charges that he'd used steroids when the two played together in Oakland, Big Mac said simply, "Once and for all, I did not use steroids or any other illegal substance." Now, under oath, McGwire's de facto invocation of his constitutional right to avoid self-incrimination was the most shocking, demoralizing thing to come out of the hearings. Here's how he explained why he refused to answer:

> Asking me, or any other player, to answer questions about who took steroids in front of television cameras will not solve his problem. If a player answers no, he simply will not be believed. If he answers yes, he risks public scorn and endless government investigations. My lawyers have advised me that I cannot answer these questions without

jeopardizing my friends, my family or myself. I intend to follow their advice.

That McGwire didn't just flat-out deny using steroids stunned one of his biggest supporters. "I was surprised by it," Cardinals manager Tony La Russa told the *New York Times* the day after McGwire's nondenial. "He's made a statement where he's denied it. I thought it was a great time for him to make that same statement. He had the biggest stage of all to say it and it looked to me like he was coached in the other direction and it surprised me."

And a lot of Big Mac's most loyal fans, as well.

Let's assume for the sake of discussion that Mark McGwire—tremendously respected and loved as a player, a cinch first-ballot Hall of Famer, the almost single-handed savior of baseball in the late 1990s—did use illegal, performance-enhancing steroids during that period. Mind you, at the time of his appearance before the congressional committee, there was no proof that he had ever done so, only uncorroborated accusations made by a former teammate in dire financial straits who had recently published a self-serving "confessional" book. Even so, McGwire had to know he was going to be convicted in the court of public opinion the minute he uttered the words, "I'm not here to talk about the past."

How did Mark get himself into this mess? I think I know. I think Mark and a lot of players bought into a mindset that prevailed in major league baseball for over a decade. That mindset had five components: (1) it's my body, and I'm willing to take on the health risk for huge financial rewards; (2) it's illegal, maybe, but it's not like crack or heroin; (3) it's not against any baseball rule; (4) a lot of the other guys are doing it; and (5) there's no testing policy, so I'll never get caught.

Clear thinking? Looking back, no. But I can see how it must have seemed so at the time.

Look, I'm not making excuses for Mark McGwire, who's certainly capable of speaking for himself, or for any other players who might have used steroids and then denied doing so. I'm merely expressing the reality of life in the big leagues during this period.

The congressional hearing was the wake-up call that baseball needed. The suits who run the game and the players who play it were forced to recognize that they had to do something, and do it fast. The implicit threat of government action combined with the reaction of the people who really own the game—the fans—finally got baseball off the dime. Suddenly everybody in the baseball establishment, from Commissioner Bud Selig and the owners to MLBPA Executive Director Donald Fehr and the union, was scrambling to put teeth in a Mickey Mouse drug policy.

Over the course of the summer, Selig reiterated his support of an escalating 50–100–Life penalty structure for players who tested positive for steroids: a 50-game suspension for the first positive test, a 100-game suspension for the second, a lifetime suspension for the third. Fehr, meanwhile, hinted that the union would support a stronger (though undefined) policy in the future.

So, did the two sides head immediately to the bargaining table to hammer out a new drug policy? No. They couldn't possibly have thought that the issue would blow away, but they clearly didn't want to deal with such unsavory business in the middle of the baseball season.

But just to make sure that they didn't forget, various members of the House of Representatives and the Senate made it abundantly clear that if baseball didn't take meaningful action to curb steroid abuse, the Federal Government would.

On July 15, 2005, Rafael Palmeiro became just the fourth player in major league history—Willie Mays, Hank Aaron, and Eddie

Murray are the other three—to join the 3,000–500 Club. The requirements for membership: 3,000 career hits *and* 500 home runs. (That explains why it's so exclusive.) As all three other members of the 3,000–500 Club were first-ballot Hall of Famers, Palmeiro's HOF credentials now looked absolutely rock-solid.

But something happened on Raffy's way to Cooperstown. On August 1, 137 days after swearing under oath that he had never used steroids, Palmeiro became the first player with Hall of Fame credentials in major league history to be suspended for having tested positively for steroid use. The anabolic steroid in question, a source inside the Commissioner's Office subsequently leaked to the press, was stanozolol, which medical experts say is easy to detect in a drug test because there is no known screening agent for it. According to Dr. Gary Wadler of NYU, an expert on drug use by athletes, stanozolol taken in pill form can linger in the body and be detected for up to a month; injected, it can be detected for up to several months.

Palmeiro was suspended for ten days by the Commissioner's Office, but he got life in prison from the public. A mild sentence, unless you count the beating his legacy and reputation took.

And you should.

This was a sad story for Palmeiro and for baseball. For him, the whole affair called into question his integrity, diminished his professional accomplishments in the public mind, and cast a cloud over his legacy that's not likely ever to go away. For the game, it blew the dark cloud of steroids directly back over it, and over all the players who had been suspected and whispered about.

Maybe worse, it put even more credence to Jose Canseco's story.

Perhaps this is a good place to pose an obvious but easily overlooked question: Do steroids guarantee success? More specifically, can steroids turn a poor hitter into a great one?

Absolutely not! There is no correlation between the ability to hit a baseball and the addition of forty pounds of lean muscle mass.

If you can't hit a curve at 180 pounds, you're not going to be able to hit it at 220. A great hitter at 180 will still be a great hitter at 220, but no greater *in terms of his ability to put his bat on the ball.* What's different is the increase in bat speed and leverage—and hence, in power—that accompanies the new muscle mass. And power is the ticket to the pot of gold. The home run is king. Chicks dig the long ball. (You knew I would say that.) And so did everybody else in baseball's Boom-Boom Years.

Players of the Steroid Era were a product of their time and of the temptations it offered. The owners, the players union, the Commissioner's Office, the media, and even the fans share the responsibility for steroid usage because we gave it our tacit approval. How long has the possibility, then the probability, then the certainty of widespread steroid use been whispered about, hinted at, winked at in the media? You think guys as smart as Donald Fehr and Bud Selig didn't suspect anything back in 1996, 1997, 1998? Did they really think guys were just pumping a lot more iron? Did they ever bother to compare trading card pictures of guys in, say, 1993 with their cards in 1999?

C'mon, let's be real.

Remember the scene in the great movie classic *Casablanca* where the police chief is ordered by the Nazi commandant to shut down Rick's, the nightclub with a not-so-private casino owned by Humphrey Bogart? The chief appears at the casino entrance and proclaims that "I am shocked, *shocked,* to discover that there is gambling going on in this establishment." Before the words are out of his mouth, the casino manager steps up and hands the chief his cut of the evening's take.

What I'm saying is that, sure, the players who got mixed up in steroids have to bear the responsibility for their actions. They're grown-ups. They knew what they were doing. But don't let the Commissioner's Office and players union off the hook. They're

responsible for running baseball and protecting the players, respectively. And they looked the other way. So did the media, who were
in clubhouses every day and saw what was happening. And while
we're doling out responsibility, where were we, the fans, while all
this was going down? Yeah, I'm including myself here. I know that
in 1998 I was thrilled by the Mac-Sammy home run race. As I said
earlier, it brought me back to the game. But . . .

Did I hear rumors of steroid use?

Yes.

Did I push hard to find out if there was anything to those rumors?

No.

Did anyone else in baseball?

No.

The "juicing" of the game over the last fifteen years has left a major
stain on baseball's cherished history. What about the record books?
Should they be altered or annotated to accurately reflect the impact of the Steroid Era on the game's cherished history? Should
McGwire, Sosa, Bonds, and all of those hitting home runs at record
levels from 1995 through 2004 have an asterisk placed next to seasons when combined home runs jumped by 25 percent over a base
period, say, 1985–94?

Nonsense.

Think about it. If you're going to start passing out asterisks,
where would you start? After every home run a guy hit after he mys-
teriously gained, say, twenty pounds (on his way to forty) of lean
muscle mass? Why not fifteen? Or twenty-five? And if you were to
do that, why stop there? Why not go back to Babe Ruth's career,
and dock him a home run for every one he hit out after spending
the night before knocking down a few illegal beers? (Hey, most of
his dingers came during Prohibition, remember?)

Okay, okay—I know it's not the same thing. But I would be flabbergasted if any records set during the Steroid Era would ever be stricken from the record books or qualified in any way. Numbers don't lie. People, yes, but not numbers.

Nonetheless, one has to wonder if Barry Bonds could have hit 73 home runs in Hank Aaron's era, or if Aaron could have hit 73 in today's game. I know the answer. Bonds would have been as good as Aaron then, and Aaron would have been as good as Bonds now. Players are products of their generations. Their performances are affected by the elements in their lives. Both of these men were destined for greatness, no matter what the era. True baseball fans will focus on the level of achievement needed for greatness in a particular era before weighing in. If I had a spare pedestal, I'd put Barry and Hank right up there together, side by side, as the two greatest power hitters of all time.

To date—and I'm writing these words in November 2005—nine major league players have tested positive for steroid use and have been suspended. Palmeiro was the only high-profile player among them. None of the nine has admitted to use or offered details of the process. Over the winter before the 2005 season began, Jason Giambi allegedly admitted in grand jury testimony that he had used steroids several years before.

Four other stars—McGwire, Sosa, Bonds, Sheffield—have been implicated by rumor and innuendo as steroid users. None has admitted to knowingly injecting, ingesting, or applying an illegal steroid. None has tested positive for steroid use. None has been disciplined by Major League Baseball. And yet all live under a fog of suspicion that only seems to increase in density.

So what do we have as concrete evidence? As of November 2005, very little. Until a major league star of the Steroid Era—other than someone with the motive of financial gain—comes forward to educate us, we remain in the dark. And I suspect we're likely to stay that way.

As for baseball's history, my suggestion is to recognize and honor those who shattered the most hallowed record in sports, the individual season home run mark. No asterisks. No annotations. Simply salute McGwire's 70 and Bonds's 73 as products of strength, timing, talent, and a mind-staggering work ethic—because all those qualities were abundantly present when they accomplished their prodigious feats.

But in honoring individual achievement, be mindful of the era. In his book *Juicing the Game,* Howard Bryant quotes Jeff Horrigan, a *Boston Herald* reporter: "There were no rules. Players are like children. They push everything as far as they can until someone stops them. Everyone did whatever they wanted . . . I blame the era, I don't blame the man."

Unfortunately, whatever the game chooses, the men who have starred in these roles will never have the joy of being recognized as legitimate record setters by fans. Steroid use, confirmed or not, will forever be linked to their careers. No matter where they go, people will second-guess their accomplishments. Maybe this is penalty enough. The story and the stain it has left on the game are so big that maybe the answer is to just leave judgment to the highest court—the court of public opinion.

On November 15, 2005, the Commissioner of Baseball and the Major League Baseball Players Association announced their agreement on a new, tougher—*much* tougher—set of penalties for steroid use: for the first positive test, a 50-game suspension; for the second, 100 games; and for the third, lifetime suspension (with the right to petition for reinstatement after two years). Selig got the penalty structure he came out in favor of after the March hearing—50–100–Life—because he had Fehr and the MLBPA over a barrel, and everybody knew it.

Senators John McCain and Jim Bunning had introduced a bill in the Senate that would have taken control of the steroids issue out of baseball's hands. It was a case of act or be acted on. Baseball acted.

We're now moving into the 2006 baseball season, with a more

educated eye on the past fifteen years of confusion. The players have slimmed down, the offensive explosion seems to have abated, and fans are happy. This may be naive, but I feel that "juicing" with steroids in baseball is over. Given the lingering presence of certain steroids in the body after use has been terminated, more positive test results may come along to shock us.

What surprised a lot of people close to baseball—including yours truly—was the inclusion in MLB's new drug policy of penalties for players who test positive for amphetamines. They're much less severe than the penalties for players who test positive for steroids: first positive test for amphetamines, mandatory follow-up testing; second positive test, 25-game suspension; third positive test, 80-game suspension; fourth positive test, penalty at the commissioner's discretion, including the possibility of a lifetime ban. Less severe, yes, but with possibly far greater implications for the game than the crackdown against steroids. Why? For the simple reason that amphetamine use in baseball is both far more common and has been going on a lot longer than steroid abuse.

The next performance-enhancing drug that baseball must deal with is HGH (Human Growth Hormone). Like steroids, HGH builds muscle mass. Unlike steroids, HGH can only be detected with a blood test. Peeing in a cup is one thing; a needle in the arm once a month is another. I suspect forging an agreement with the MLBPA on blood testing will be difficult. So putting blood testing for HGH on the bargaining table prematurely could slow down implementation of the new steroid policy—perhaps even derail it. My recommendation: Give the new steroid policy (testing *and* penalties) a chance to work (say, one year), and then take on HGH.

If the last fifteen years have taught us anything, it's that baseball must be more vigilant, more aware, and more proactive in defending the game's fundamental integrity.

After all, players will never stop looking for an edge.

9 Better Than Ever

Hitters today are flat-out better than ever.

That's no typo. Your eyes aren't playing tricks on you. The classic "back in the day," old school guy is saying, unequivocally, that hitters today are better than hitters in any other era in baseball history. Some of today's best hitters could flourish in any generation, but the entire crop could out-hit a comparable group from any previous era.

Now, when you come up for air, and after what I promise you is a demanding technical analysis on why this is so, I'm betting you'll agree with me. Getting my cronies from the 1970s and 1980s to agree? That's another story.

Before you jump in, though, let me first assure you that your not-so-humble author knows what he's talking about. Why? Because I lived it, every aspect of hitting—the good and the bad, the thick and the thin, the heights and the depths. What other baseball player do you know who could list the following on his résumé:

- Hit 38 home runs with 80 Ks one season.
- Hit 38 home runs with 170 Ks another season.
- Hit .316 one season.
- Hit .196 another season.
- Hit 4 home runs in one game.
- Struck out 4 times on 12 pitches in another game.

There are some great hitting coaches who were tremendous hitters—Hal McRae, Jim Rice, Bill Robinson, and Don Mattingly come quickly to mind—but none was ever as bad as me at my worst. And there are some great hitting coaches who were only so-so hitters: Charlie Lau heads this group.

But I submit that no hitting coach in history has known the highs and lows I experienced with a bat in my hands in the majors. As a player, I studied swing mechanics to the extent that I actually hindered my own development as a hitter. I experimented with every stance, position in the box, grip pressure, swing plane, stride distance, and size of bat known to man. I know the mechanics of pull hitting and straightaway hitting. I know about pitch anticipation and staying inside the ball. I know about the psychology of pressure at-bats with the game on the line, and I know about the difference between hitting with men on base and with the bases empty. I've developed a theory on at-bats when your team's ahead and when you're behind. I know good, solid adjustment techniques for all situations. I know all this because I lived it every day for twenty years, and I'm still studying it.

So when I tell you today's hitters are better than ever, you can take it to the bank.

Let's start with the obvious: bigger, stronger, faster. That's become a sports cliché because it's true: Today's athletes are bigger, stronger, faster than ever before. When I played I was considered big at six-two, 195 pounds. Nowadays, when I stand by the batting cage in spring training, I'm about average size. Ballplayers today are bigger. And bigger, if you're in shape—and believe me, today's guys are—means more powerful. *Much* more powerful.

Today's players grew up with a different mindset toward training than ballplayers from earlier eras. Physical conditioning and nutrition play a huge role in this generation's lifestyle. The weight room is always crowded in today's baseball world—in college, in the minors, and especially in the big leagues. Most big leaguers combine in-season regimens with off-season training that's even more rigorous. Many have their own personal professional trainers. Most are knowledgeable about nutrition and pay careful attention to their diets.

Let me assure you that John Kruk's famous "Hey, lady—I'm not an athlete, I'm a baseball player" bullshit has no place in the game today.

Sixty years ago, maybe one in twenty major league hitters—if that many—gave his physical condition any thought. Off-season conditioning programs didn't exist, unless you count chopping wood or occasionally squeezing a handgrip. (You have to cut them some slack: After all, most had to take off-season jobs to keep food on the table.)

Thirty years ago—my era—maybe one in five hitters lifted weights, and that would have been in the off-season only. Then in the 1980s, the fitness boom exploded. As health clubs, training equipment, and training coaches came into play, players saw that conditioning and strength training could increase strength and prolong careers.

My career was extended, and I remained one of the best in the game from 1980 through 1987, because of my trainers, Gus Hoefling and Pat Croce. You wouldn't believe the off-season training program I went through with Gus. Some of it bordered on torture, as did Pat's. It was no big deal to bail out and vomit in the middle of a conditioning set. Try twenty-five push-ups and twenty-five sit-ups, then twenty push-ups and twenty sit-ups, then fifteen and fifteen, on down to zero—on the clock. That was part of Gus's *warm-up*.

Pat introduced me to the thirty-minute aerobic training circuit as a warm-up: five minutes each at high speed on bike, treadmill, rower, arm ergometer, climber, and jump rope. Make it through that and *then* start your workout.

So in the 1980s, I saw serious benefits to training. It became a way of life, a necessary element of being a baseball player. As players entered the 1990s, the fitness boom accelerated, with a higher percentage of players doing weight training year-round. The 1990s also saw the beginning of stricter attention to diet and the use of dietary supplements.

Coaching and training young hitters has also developed into a popular science. Kids today, starting in Little League, are exposed to coaching as never before. Just as there are personal trainers, there are hitting coaches and hitting schools everywhere. My summer league coach in Dayton, Ted Mills, runs a hitting school. We have the Tommy Hutton Baseball Academy near my home in South Florida and Bucky Dent's Baseball School a little farther south. I've even started a hitting school called the School of Hard Knocks. Kids whose parents can afford it get professional coaching, with top-flight equipment, before entering high school.

As young hitters progress, monitored training and practice more than keep pace. Game experience is double what it was thirty years ago. There are cages and modern playing facilities everywhere. Families build their lives around a kid's baseball training. A college player today takes double the batting practice swings I got as a college player and triple the number of game at-bats. The math's pretty simple: more practice reps + more game at-bats = better hitters.

In the big leagues today, all hitters have a daily routine that includes more than 100 practice swings off the tee or front side toss (short underhand toss from a coach). And if he opts for extra BP, a hitter may get up to 200 reps before a game. It's all there for the taking.

In my day, there was no such thing as a pre-BP warm-up routine unless you went off on your own with a tee. Today, major league hitting coaches have the cage ready hours before regularly scheduled batting practice. All ballparks now have hitting "laboratories" where hitters can pick the drills and teaching aids of their choice, as well as have a coach on call ready to throw. The indoor batting cage is used every day, not just on rainy days, as was the case years ago. Hitting's not quite a 24/7 deal for big leaguers serious about their craft, but it's heading that way.

Every team has a video technician who travels with them. He sets up a station in the clubhouse specifically for daily video study. Players watch that day's starter in his last outing to prepare for the game, or they pull specific personal at-bats to diagnose problems. Stadiums have cameras mounted on both dugouts to capture different angles. All games are taped and broken down so each player has his own reel. A hitter goes to the video technician, tell him the game he wants to see, and *zap!* there it is on the screen.

The aluminum bat used throughout amateur ball also helps develop better hitting skills. It's lighter, with a larger sweet spot, and unbreakable. Young hitters learn they don't have to commit early to the pitch; this reinforces waiting and identifying the location and movement of the ball. Add to that the fear college and high school pitchers develop of pitching inside, and you have young hitters being served a steady diet of pitches to the outer side of the plate. Watch a college game and notice how many hitters stand close to the plate or open to it and stride toward the hitting area without fear of inside pitches. This helps develop a straightaway hitting style and makes for a better, more consistent hitter.

As a little boy at the local playground, I started out learning to pull the ball. There was a practical reason for this: In our games, we never had enough guys to have a right fielder , so you were out if you hit a ball to right. We didn't even have a left-handed kid on the block, so the grass in right field was beautiful. I didn't even know right field existed. The pitcher tried to throw the ball inside so we could jack it to left. All the talk was always about how far someone hit a ball toward Fieldstone Drive, beyond left field. So I grew up a dead pull hitter.

In high school and college, we were taught to hit the ball "out front" of the plate. Today, sound hitting theory stresses hitting "over the plate," letting the ball get deeper into the hitting area. Few major leaguers today are dead pull hitters. In fact, today's young hitters are the opposite of most hitters of my era.

Through the 1980s, power hitters pulled the ball, while singles hitters sprayed it to all fields. That was the rule. Natural straightaway hitters with home run power were rare. The spray hitters and opposite-field hitters were mostly Latino players. The Alous, Roberto Clemente, Orlando Cepeda, and Tony Perez all had natural opposite-field power, putting them ahead of their time. Only one American-born hitter from my era stands out in my memory as an opposite-field hitter with power: Bob Watson. And his home run production was curtailed by the Astrodome.

Combining power with a high batting average was relatively unusual. My career BA was .267, a perfectly respectable figure for a top power hitter in my time. Not so today. Albert Pujols, the best right-handed power hitter in the game, jacks 40-plus homers *and* hits .340 while doing it. His counterpart in the AL, Manny Ramirez, also combines big power with a career .314 BA.

The downside of aluminum bats, of course, is that it's hard for high school and college hitters to make the adjustment when they turn pro. The wooden bat is heavier and will break. The hitter has the burden of centering the ball on a smaller sweet spot, meaning his hitting mechanics need to be more precise. If they're not, he's vulnerable to the pitch inside that he used to handle easily with the metal bat.

The battle between hitter and pitcher is the centerpiece of the game. The pitcher wins that battle most often against hitters who feel insecure about inside fastballs. A hitter insecure about his ability to handle inside heat tends to make mechanical adjustments to guard that area, such as opening the front shoulder or committing the hands forward—or both. The two adjustments "feel" like the right thing to do, but together they are the root cause of every slump in history. Fear of being beaten by the inside fastball makes a hitter easy prey for a pitcher who can follow a ball inside with a strike on the outside of the plate.

Most young hitters don't make the adjustment from metal to wood. But if a young hitter successfully learns to use his new weapon and retains his sound, straightaway style, he'll have a much superior hitting foundation to young hitters of my era and more upside than a hitter whose instinct is to pull everything. Pujols, Alex Rodriguez, Manny Ramirez, Scott Rolen, Derrek Lee, Miguel Cabrera, and Carlos Delgado are the best straightaway power hitters today. There's nothing that grabs a pitcher's attention faster than a hitter with power to all fields.

My first seven years, my natural instinct was to try to pull everything—the old Dayton playground stroke. That made me easy to pitch to in clutch situations. The pitcher always knew what I was going to try to do. Low and outside? Pull it. High and inside? Pull it. Away? Pull it. In? Pull it. Dangerous? Yes. Consistent? No. It wasn't until I discovered a remedy to make myself a straightaway hitter—that is, someone who made pitchers more respectful and defenses more honest. My remedy: stand farther from the plate, stride forward toward the plate, and look to hit the away pitch to right center.

• • •

Thirty years ago, pitchers tried to get batters out by making a good pitch to the outside half of the plate that would induce a fly ball to center or to the opposite field. Most pitchers, except for the strike-out guys like Koufax, Gibson, Seaver, and Ryan, wanted the hitter to hit the ball, put it in play. Back then, all parks had a field where fly balls went to die. Today? Not so many. Getting today's power hitter to hit a fly ball, *any* fly ball, is a risky proposition. Today's pitchers—most of them, anyway—operate from a mindset of "pitching away from the bat."

My experience managing the Class A Clearwater Threshers in 2004, in a home park (Bright House Networks Field) built to almost exactly the same specs as Citizens Bank Park in Philly, taught me to cringe at every fly ball the opposing team hit. That happens when your pitcher gives up a 360-foot fly and the hitter goes into his trot. Like most other pitchers in the minors and majors alike, my guys quickly came to fear the bat. They felt they needed to trick the hitter on every pitch—do anything, really, except challenge him. The result: deep counts, pitching from behind, higher pitch counts, earlier fatigue—and losses.

Perversely, this philosophy of fear is hard on today's hitters in one respect: It makes it harder for them to look for or anticipate pitches. Thirty years ago, I knew what I'd see on a 2–0 count: fastball away—you against me, baby. Today, it could be a two-seamer, four-seamer, splitter, change-up, cutter—just about *anything* but straight fastball away. Having to look for anything at any time is tougher. No sitting on the fastball away, like in the old days. Pitchers today have to do *something* to compensate for 350-feet power alleys. The fact that hitters are still knocking down the fences is testimony to how much better today's hitters are than in my day.

Hitters nowadays see the entire field as one big power alley. Hitting in a small park makes a good hitter better because he knows he only has to center the ball on the bat and it will go. Unlike hitters of other eras, most of whom needed to pull the ball to hit it over the fence, guys today feast off the opposite field.

One other thing: Pitchers today fear the bat, but most hitters don't fear the ball. That's because pitchers don't routinely employ the brushback as a normal part of their arsenal. Thirty years ago, it was part of the game to get knocked down by the pitcher. A knockdown told the hitter that the pitcher respected him. Hitters had labels: "Just knock him down and he's done." Or, in the case of a Frank Robinson: "Whatever you do, *don't* knock him down or you'll never get him out." (That's the label we all wanted.)

Pitching up and in to deter aggressive hitters went away when the umpires were given control of that aspect of the game. If a batter doesn't have in the back of his mind that he could get one in the neck for taking liberties with the pitcher's sense of what's rightfully his, he starts the at-bat with an advantage. It's like starting a golf match one-up before you even tee off.

Back in the day, the pitcher knew that he had to induce some measure of "ball fear" in the hitter's mind. Prior to 1990, the players policed their own game for the most part, and there were actually fewer instances of the hitter-pitcher confrontation getting out of hand. The knockdown pitch was a routine part of the game. Nowadays the umpires are so quick to issue an official warning on pitches that come close that a pitcher might as well not bother. Taking away the knockdown pitch from the pitcher's arsenal has tipped the game's basic battle in favor of the hitter.

Pitchers used to believe as an article of faith that they had to own the outside corner in order to feed their families. Today, hitters are just as sure that it belongs to them. Imagine a Manny Ramirez or a Gary Sheffield lunging over the plate while fouling off a Bob Gibson slider, low and away. Next pitch, no matter what the count, Manny or Gary is on his back, I guarantee it. And the next time he steps in against Gibby, he'll think twice about diving over the plate.

One last observation concerning the "fear factor" that's so critical in the hitter-pitcher confrontation, and it has to do with Roger Clemens. Do you think the Rocket, who is only the greatest right-hand pitcher in baseball history—maybe the greatest *pitcher*—would have been half as great, even with all his speed and stuff, if hitters had ever felt *comfortable* standing in against him? No way. Roger's best pitch isn't a pitch at all: it's the fear he induces in guys standing 60 feet, 6 inches away from him.

Your typical pitcher today is like a boxer hoping to finesse his way through a match with a back-alley brawler. If he bobs and weaves through five or six innings while giving up only three or four runs, he can head to the dugout and be congratulated by his teammates on a good outing: "Way to keep us in the game!" There's even a stat for it now. A "quality start" is one in which you give up "only" three earned runs in six innings—a 4.50 ERA! (Wonder what Steve Carlton in his prime would have thought about a start like that?)

That sounds like I'm knocking today's pitchers, but I'm not. Actually, in most of the newer stadiums today, three or four runs in six innings *is* a good outing. Problem is, this approach has become the norm in all stadiums.

Today, if your ERA's under 4.00, you're a valued commodity, probably a number two or three starter in a good rotation. By the standards of 1985 and earlier, of course, a 4.00 ERA marked you as a fringe pitcher with a short major league career. But so what? Times change. Fans over forty are hard-wired to believe that the game they watched growing up, and the game I played from 1972 to 1989, was the only way to play baseball. Not so. There's nothing inherently wrong with a 4.00 ERA leading a league or a 16-win season earning Cy Young votes—no matter how strange it might seem to us old-timers.

Most pitchers today don't go after the hitters. Nine out of ten pitches are aimed at a corner of the plate. Fastball on outside corner: 0–1. Slider outside: 1–1. Sinker inside: 2–1. Slider away: 3–1. Years ago, the 3–1 pitch would be a fastball aimed right down the middle. Today, it's a two-seamer or a four-seamer at a corner. A 3–1 count today turns into a walk more often than ever before. Pitchers routinely hit the 100-pitch mark between the fifth and sixth. So they end up working fewer innings than guys in my era did while throwing just as many pitches, perhaps more.

Maybe it's that they're more afraid than their predecessors of what happens when ball meets bat.

Or maybe it's just that they're smarter.

My brain works overtime on the subject of hitting. I studied it as a player. I became one of the best in the game at it. I coach it. I wrote a book about it (*The Mike Schmidt Study*). And I'm still searching for the truth. My journey started with a very limited understanding and ended in the Hall of Fame. And yet, when it comes to thinking about hitting, I'm nowhere near done.

I started out as an insecure, right-handed pull hitter with dangerous power, but I could also be an easy out. Eventually, I taught myself to be a confident contact hitter with power to all fields and a league leader in on-base percentage. I lived the experience. I know both sides. I'm familiar with the peaks and valleys. Early on, I won a couple of MVP awards, but not until midway through my career—when I won a third MVP—did I finally become the most valuable hitter on my own team. And I did that by studying the art of hitting.

All this is by way of establishing my credentials to talk about the best hitter in baseball history: Barry Bonds.

No player in baseball history has received more intense scrutiny, in the media and from fans, than Barry. More words have been written about him and spouted on TV and radio than about any other player. A huge number of those words, of course, have been negative, highly critical—and purely speculative.

Did Barry Bonds use steroids? All we know—and we "know" that only from leaked grand jury testimony—is that he admitted using a cream given to him by his trainer that, unknown to Bonds, contained a steroid. Is that the whole story? I don't know. Will we ever know the whole story? Probably not. Will the rumors and speculation and innuendos ever cease? Not a chance.

But try to set all that aside. Try to focus solely on what Barry Bonds does with a bat in his hands. Ready? Okay, so let me outline the seven factors that, in my view, make Barry *the best hitter in baseball history*—period.

1. He's left-handed. Of the top ten hitters for average all-time, eight are left-handed. (Rogers Hornsby and Ed Delahanty are the only righties.) Left-handed hitters are closer to first base, and 75 percent of the pitchers they face are right-handers. This eliminates the fear factor in three-quarters of their at-bats. That's huge.

2. He's unselfish. Bonds understands that the fear opposing pitchers have of him creates an unusually high number of opportunities for hitters around him. He could easily widen his hitting zone, put more balls in play, and—hard as it is to fathom—hit more home runs. *But he'd also make more outs.* Any inning in which he bats is a potential rally because he gets on base more often than any other active player in baseball. He has a .442 career OBP through 2005, the sixth best all-time. And he's number one and two in the all-time single-season OBP rankings with an astonishing .609 in 2004 and .582 in 2002. (In case you were wondering, the number three slot is held by Ted Williams, who had a .553 OBP in 1941 when he was just twenty-two. Oh, yeah—that was also the year he hit .406.) Bonds, who holds

four of the top eleven single-season OBPs in ML history, fashioned them all after his thirty-sixth birthday. What's the saying about fine wine?

3. He can wait longer to identify the pitch and react to it deeper in the hitting box than any power hitter ever. Strength, mechanics, exceptional eyesight, choking up on the bat, and confidence based on experience are the keys to his ability to stay back. The longer a hitter can wait, the better his chances of hitting *his* pitch, not swinging at the *pitcher's* pitch.

4. His stroke is short, quick, and level through the ball—and incredibly powerful. He uses the big muscles of his trunk in a tight, compact fashion, as if he were standing and turning in a barrel. No wasted motion. Always in balance. Maximum torque. Combining all that with exceptional hand speed and strength means he can catch up to any fastball, in any location, at any time, against any pitcher. Bonds can be looking for a breaking ball and hit an inside fastball out of the park. A few swings today are as powerful; none is quicker.

5. He knows he intimidates every pitcher he faces. As so much of the pitcher-hitter confrontation is psychological, he enjoys a huge edge the second he steps into the batter's box.

6. He rarely hurts himself with wrong guesses. He actually figures every pitch to him is going to be a ball, so he never looks for a fat pitch to hit on 2–0 or 3–1. His home runs come from reaction, not anticipation.

7. Finally—and this may seem trivial, but it's not—Bonds takes full advantage of subtle changes in the rules of the game over the past decade. He knows, for instance, that the strike zone has shrunk to the size of a laptop; he has the amply deserved rep of knowing that zone better than the man squatting behind the catcher. Bonds wears an elbow guard, which twenty years ago would not have been allowed. It shields his front side from

inside fastballs, functioning as a security blanket that makes him more comfortable at the plate.

What all this comes down to is pretty simple: Barry Bonds is a run-producing machine because he makes fewer outs than anyone in the game. He makes fewer outs because he swings the bat fewer times. He swings the bat fewer times because pitchers throw him mostly balls. He is able to "not" swing because his quickness allows him to wait back and identify pitches outside his zone. He accepts the fact that he'll have fewer pitches to hit because he knows the value of not making an out, understands how that affects his team's ability to score runs, and is patient enough to trust he'll make the most of the few opportunities he gets.

The bottom line: Barry Bonds is in complete command of his hitting box.

The "hitting box" is a space approximately 30 inches high, 20 inches wide, and 20 inches deep. This is the area where the batter intends to make contact with the ball. As the ball travels toward this box, the hitter maneuvers into the swing or reject position. This position is crucial. A hitter who gets to this position off balance or too abruptly or with a flinch forward of the hands has committed prematurely to swinging or taking because he got a false reading on speed and movement. The pitcher's job, through change of speeds, location, spin, and arm speed, is to trick a hitter into losing feel for his hitting box. Bonds seldom falls into this trap, and when he does, he can make a lightning-quick adjustment.

Most hitters, most of the time, make the swing/take decision too soon. They're influenced by the pitcher's deception into committing before the ball reaches their hitting box. Hitters unfamiliar with the location of their hitting box, and with little feel for how to use it, adjust too slowly and waste at-bats. They tend to be inconsistent and usually succeed only against one-speed pitchers.

A hitter who allows the pitch to get to his hitting box and makes contact is far more likely to hit the ball hard because he's letting the ball travel deep, almost over the plate. To hit to the opposite field with authority, you need to allow the ball to travel over the outer portion of the plate. Also, a swing approaching the ball from slightly above yields the highest percentage of line drives upon contact.

A hitter in control of his hitting box gets himself into a balanced, relaxed "decision" position as the ball approaches. He trusts his fundamentals. He's less apt to swing at bad pitches. He makes fewer easy outs and forces starters out of games early, which means facing middle relievers sooner, which translates into more runs, which gives you more games in the W column. Sounds simple, doesn't it?

So how come the pitcher wins 65 to 70 percent of the confrontations with the very best hitters? Well, it's just flat impossible to arrive at a perfect hitting position every time the ball enters the hitting box. It's also impossible to deliver a quick, short downswing every time; the temptation to try to lift the ball is too great. And, of course, it's impossible to control the ball after it leaves the bat. Too often, somebody catches it.

The good news is that a hitter *can* learn to understand that developing a quick, short downswing—and learning to trust it—opens up an entire new world. He *can* find his hitting box, one deeper over the plate. He *can* learn to hit fastballs straightaway. He *can* learn to hit or reject off-speed pitches from a balanced "decision" position. And he *can* learn how to let the game come to him.

The way Barry Bonds does.

To some degree, I can relate directly to Barry Bonds. I lived with insecurities, and reacted to them in similar fashion, when I was a player. I was never the likable hero Phillies fans wanted me to be. I alienated many people with my constant focus on my needs. I was only satisfied when *my* world was running smoothly, and I came to expect my teammates and coaches to help make that happen.

A successful team is often built around a dominant individual, but only rarely around a player who transcends the team's sport to become the greatest in the sport's history. Michael Jordan. Wayne Gretzky. Jim Brown. The list isn't that long. And Barry Bonds is on it.

Managing your world in a team sport environment while on your way to the top of the mountain as an individual is a monumental task. There's just so much exposure, so much pressure from external sources, so much off-the-field stuff to deal with on a daily, season-long basis. And Barry, by all the "good guy" standards, has failed on that front, especially in his dealings with the media.

Been there, done that. Looking back, I give myself a B– in the Good Guy Department. At least I *wanted* to be liked. I cared about the issues and lives of my teammates and coaches, and I'm secure in knowing I left the game with hundreds of good friends. I was aware of my selfish ways, but I also understood that I couldn't be somebody I wasn't. I couldn't be a Tug McGraw or a Gary Matthews, guys I admired for their outgoing friendliness.

(And I couldn't be a contemporary of mine who in many ways was the exact opposite of me—a fellow by the name of George Brett. Charming, lovable, adored by fans, a Hall of Famer, and a true gamer. Also a pretty good third baseman, I hear.)

Sharp, concise visualization and precise, repetitive execution require total concentration, intense self-absorption, and intense internalization. This can be tough for outsiders to handle. To stay at the top, to perform to my standards, meant sacrifice, not just from me but from those around me. Ask my wife, Donna, who had to put up with my moods, my media failures, and a loss of privacy. Ask the two coaches, Bobby Wine and Mike Ryan, who blew out their shoulders throwing me batting practice. Ask the Phillies traveling secretary (a suite on the road), the Vet's grounds crew (a perfect batter's box), or clubhouse men in other towns (the same locker every year). I depended a great deal on the patience and dedication of all those people.

Barry Bonds is a friend. I have played against him, done public appearances with him, interviewed him, hit my 500th home run over him, and admired him for his recent accomplishments. My suggestion to Barry, and this comes from personal experience, would be to make the needs of people around him more important than his own. That would create some good Karma, something Barry—like the rest of us—needs.

It might even make people *want* him to break Hank Aaron's HR record.

WALK-OFF HOMER WINS
1961 LITTLE LEAGUE
TOURNAMENT! It doesn't get
any better than this—part I.
(COURTESY OF THE AUTHOR)

Puerto Rico, 1973: If you
hit .196 your rookie year,
you damned well better
be the MVP of the Puerto
Rican League All-Star Game.
(COURTESY OF THE AUTHOR)

Think times haven't changed?
Between us in 1975, Dick Allen
and I hit a grand total of 50
homers. (© THE TOPPS COMPANY)

The 10-20-30 Club *(from left):* me, Larry Bowa, and Dave Cash. One of the best infields in history. Will those uniforms ever come back? (COURTESY OF THE PHILADELPHIA PHILLIES)

Pete Rose joined the Phillies in 1979 to lead us to a World Championship— and the following season, he did just that. (COURTESY OF THE PHILADELPHIA PHILLIES)

No one enjoyed the game more than Tug McGraw. I miss you, Neighbor. (COURTESY OF THE PHILADELPHIA PHILLIES)

PHILLIES WIN 1980 WORLD SERIES! It doesn't get any better than this—part II. (COURTESY OF THE AUTHOR)

You hit 548 home runs, you go through a lot of wood. (© BETTMANN/CORBIS)

"Undercover Phil," 1985:
If they can't recognize
you, they can't boo you.
(AP PHOTO)

Unveiling my statue outside Citizens Bank Park,
Opening Day, 2004. I wish I could have had
my 8,352 career at-bats *inside* that place.
(© TIM SHAFFER/REUTERS/CORBIS)

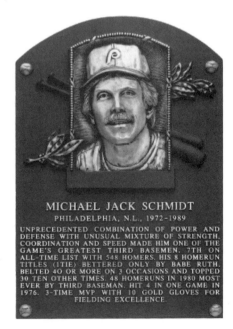

Funny, that guy looks familiar. . . .
(COURTESY OF THE MAJOR LEAGUE BASEBALL
HALL OF FAME)

MICHAEL JACK SCHMIDT
PHILADELPHIA, N.L., 1972–1989
UNPRECEDENTED COMBINATION OF POWER AND
DEFENSE WITH UNUSUAL MIXTURE OF STRENGTH,
COORDINATION AND SPEED MADE HIM ONE OF THE
GAME'S GREATEST THIRD BASEMEN. 7TH ON
ALL-TIME LIST WITH 548 HOMERS. HIS 8 HOMERUN
TITLES (1TIE) BETTERED ONLY BY BABE RUTH.
BELTED 40 OR MORE ON 3 OCCASIONS AND TOPPED
30 TEN OTHER TIMES. 48 HOMERUNS IN 1980 MOST
EVER BY THIRD BASEMAN. HIT 4 IN ONE GAME IN
1976. 3-TIME MVP WITH 10 GOLD GLOVES FOR
FIELDING EXCELLENCE.

In 1998 Sammy and Big Mac brought me—and millions of other fans—
back to baseball. (AFP/STEPHEN JAFFE)

Barry Bonds is the best hitter in baseball history—period.
(JOHN W. MCDONOUGH/SPORTS ILLUSTRATED)

"Never. Period." In March 2005, Rafael Palmeiro tells Congress that he never used steroids. Later that summer, he was suspended for ten days after testing positive for stanozolol, an anabolic steroid. (GETTY IMAGES NEWS/MARK WILSON)

Major League Baseball Players Association Executive Director Donald Fehr and Major League Baseball Commissioner Bud Selig were grilled by Congress on why baseball did not move quicker to address widespread steroid use. They didn't have very good answers. (GETTY IMAGES NEWS/ CHIP SOMODEVILLA)

Free agency can be confusing: First, Pedro Martinez leads the Red Sox to the 2004 World Championship. Next, he's all set to become a Yankee. About fifteen minutes later, he's a Met. (GETTY IMAGES SPORT/CHRIS TROTMAN)

As I discovered in 2004 as manager of the Clearwater Threshers, Class A ball is a season-long learning curve. (PHOTO BY AL MESSERSCHMIDT, COURTESY OF THE CLEARWATER THRESHERS)

Who's on third? George Brett, Brooks Robinson, and yours truly in Cooperstown, 2003. (COURTESY OF THE AUTHOR)

10 The Boom-Boom Years

Baseball is a numbers game. Always has been, always will be. In no other team sport do numbers carry so much weight, and tell you so much about performance. You know this if you've ever memorized the numbers on the back of a baseball card—and what true fan hasn't?

Best of all, numbers let you evaluate and compare players over time. Good day: 4 for 4. Bad day: 0 for 4. Good season: .300. Bad season: .225. Power hitter: 35+ HR, 100 RBI. Gap hitter: 40 doubles, 70 RBI. And so on in 2005, as it was in 1955, and as it will be in 2055.

Numbers *mean* something in baseball. That's why, if I'm going to talk about how baseball has changed since I played, I'm going to start with a few of my numbers.

In 1974, 1975, and 1976, I led the National League in home runs with 36, 38, and 38, respectively. Over in the American League in that three-year span, the home run leaders were my old teammate Dick Allen, then with the White Sox, with 32; George

Scott (Brewers) and Reggie Jackson (A's), both with 36; and Graig Nettles (Yankees), 32. Back then, 35–40 home runs added up to an outstanding power season.

Now, flash-forward to another three-year span, one picked for an obvious reason: 1998, 1999, 2000. The AL home run leaders those three years were Junior Griffey (Mariners), 56; Griffey again, 48; and Troy Glaus (Angels), 47, and in the NL, Mark McGwire (Cardinals), 70; McGwire again, 65; and Sammy Sosa (Cubs), 50.

Think about those numbers a minute. The AL and NL home run leaders in 1974–76 hit a combined total of 212 home runs. Their counterparts in 1998–2000 stroked 336. Got your calculator? That's a 63 *percent* difference.

One more point: The *combined* HR totals for the AL and NL leaders in the earlier period were 68, 74, 70. In 2001, you may recall, a fellow by the name of Barry Bonds hit 73—all by himself.

Suddenly 35–40 homers a year doesn't look so outstanding.

Think maybe the home run explosion in the late 1990s was accompanied by a comparable surge in overall hitting? Think again. The combined league batting averages in 1974–76 were .257 in the AL and .256 in the NL, vs. .268 and .265 in 1998–2000. Exclude the DH factor in the American League, and you're looking at an additional 8 to 10 points across both leagues in the latter period—a relatively modest 4 percent increase.

No, the single biggest change in baseball since my day is, indisputably, the huge jump in home runs. And that leads to two obvious questions:

What caused the Home Run Boom?

What has it done to the game?

Baseball officials say there's no difference in today's ball from twenty years ago. What the hell else can they say? The fact is, today's ball is wound a little tighter, is a little harder, has slightly flatter seams, and is a little more consistent. Not much, but enough to matter, enough to make it hotter, enough to make it travel slightly farther.

Don't believe me? Ask a pitcher. Ask *any* major league pitcher.

This is an old argument, one that always ends the same way, with fingers pointed at the old horsehide (cowhide since 1974)—and with no hard proof. Since Babe Ruth hit 54 home runs in 1920 to smash the old HR record (29, which he set in 1919) and thereby ushered in the Live Ball Era, every boost in offensive production, every jump in home run output, has been accompanied by charges that the ball has been fiddled with, purposefully, by . . . well, by whom, exactly? The manufacturers (Spalding until 1974, now Rawlings)? The Commissioner's Office? Some vast international conspiracy, devoted to the manipulation of the American psyche by cheapening the signature act of America's Game?

Stop. *Of course* the ball has gotten livelier over the last century or so. Manufacturing standards have gotten better. Quality control systems have gotten better. Materials have gotten better (especially after World War I). And usage patterns—mainly, how long a ball is kept in play—have gotten better. So why shouldn't the ball itself have gotten better?

More than anything else, merely giving hitters a fresh ball to look at changed the game. In baseball's early days, a baseball was kept in play no matter how scuffed and dirty it became. Before 1920, club owners required that foul balls hit into the stands be returned to the field and put back in play. By late afternoon on an overcast day, it's a wonder batters could see the ball, much less hit it. Only after the death of Ray Chapman on August 20, 1920, following a beaning four days earlier, did baseball decree that the umpires must keep a clean white ball in play at all times.

Every kid's love of the game starts with the ball, and I was no exception. Somewhere near the age of five, I got my first introduction to the baseball, known universally back then as the "hardball."

Getting your hands on a new hardball was a rare and treasured event, and if you had one, you guarded it like a precious jewel.

I signed my first ball in June 1970 at the College World Series, following Ohio University's first-round win over number one– ranked Southern California. Coming out of Rosenblatt Stadium in Omaha, sky-high from the victory, I was walking toward the team bus when someone stuck a ball out to me. I knew exactly where to sign it, from personal experience at the other end of the process when I was a kid at Crosley Field: just above the manufacturer's name, right on the sweet spot.

Can you imagine how many baseballs I've had in my hands in the thirty-five years since then? Maybe a hundred thousand. Maybe more. So no matter what ball manufacturers say, no matter what the Commissioner's Office says, I can tell you the baseball has gone through subtle changes in texture and size. If I can feel those changes, imagine a major league pitcher who makes his living through his "feel" of the ball?

The size of the baseball was standardized back in the 1860s. It was to weigh between 5 and 5.25 ounces, with a circumference between 9 and 9.25 inches. It was manufactured by winding yarn around a small core of cork, rubber, or similar material, then encasing the sphere in horsehide stained white with slightly raised red stitches. In 1931, a cushioned "cork" center was added, with the effect of deadening the ball slightly; and the seams were raised a bit, which allowed the pitcher a better grip on breaking balls. This ball was used until 1974, when cowhide replaced horsehide. The cowhide ball has been in use ever since—without changing, juicing, fiddling, or in any way deviating from the official specs. Or so they say.

Rawlings sends more than 700,000 balls to the majors each year. I can't even guess at the total number of balls manufactured when you include the retail market, which is affected dramatically by the memorabilia industry. (Heck, I still sign a few thousand balls a year myself.) A couple of hundred thousand of today's game balls are thrown into the stands each season like peanuts, each representing a $10 investment in marketing the game. Hang over the railing at a game today, and you have a good chance of getting a ball. In fact, kids today are programmed to expect players to throw them a souvenir ball. Also, every pitch that hits the dirt is discarded. Catchers hand the ball back to the ump if it gets near the dirt, and the ump always throws it out. Twenty years ago, slightly scuffed balls were rubbed down by an umpire and returned to play. Players were fined for throwing a $10 ball in the stands, both because of the cost of the ball and the potential liability if a fan were to get hit.

So, if the manufacturer is consistent in production and quality control, why do so many who are close to the game insist today's balls are more lively—not by a lot, maybe, but enough to have a subtle but real impact?

To me, the best judges are the current coaches, especially recently retired guys who have stayed in the game and have a firsthand look and feel for the current ball and its flight. Joe Morgan has stayed very close to the game, and he swears the current ball is harder. David Wells and Barry Zito, left-handed curveball artists, insist the ball is tighter and has lower seams.

Two summers ago, when I managed in Class A, I threw batting practice for five straight months, and I believe in my heart that the current balls are slightly tighter, and ever so slightly smaller. So while there are other significant reasons for the offensive boom of the last decade, I believe there is no question that the baseball, that little 5.25-ounce sphere we all cherish so much, is—as it always has been in a situation like this—a likely suspect.

You never forget your first time. The day I reported to the Reading Phillies of the Eastern League, my first professional assignment, there were two contracts waiting for me. One was the standard Louisville

Slugger bat deal extended to every player when he turned professional; the other was from a new company, Adirondack, a subsidiary
of Rawlings, the outfit that made the glove that I'd used since Little
League. I looked long and hard at these, because getting my name
inscribed on a custom-made bat was one of my baseball dreams.

And now it was coming true for me.

Actually, the neatest part of the dream, when your actual signature is added to a bat, comes a little way down the road, when you
get to the big leagues and if you make a big enough mark. But heck,
my name printed on a *Mickey Mantle* model? How cool was that!

The big question on that first day was, Louisville Slugger or
Adirondack?

Louisville Slugger, of course, was the gold standard in bats at
the time. All professional hitters used Louisville Sluggers. In fact,
just about all hitters everywhere used them. In Little League, I used
a 32-inch Black Beauty, with "Louisville Slugger" stamped on the
fat part of the barrel. (P.S.: I hit .737 that year.)

The bat designs we had in college were exact replicas of the
actual major league models. Today, the designs, style, weight, and
length are still created and adjusted by the player and company reps
in spring training. The hitters test different bats, and engineers tweak
them to fit the individual hitter's preferences. As the hitter becomes
more successful and better known, his autograph and associated code
number are forever locked to his model. One of the most popular
models back then was the K55 (Mickey Mantle). That model, style,
and associated number will go on till the end of time. As long as
there is baseball, there will be a Louisville Slugger K55.

During my college days at Ohio University, the day we got to
pick out our first couple of bats was like Christmas morning to a
bunch of five-year-olds. All those boxes of Louisville Sluggers in
the equipment room like so many presents under the tree! Only
one of us was allowed in the room at a time. Guys couldn't help but

pull one out of every box and feel it. We'd go, "How did Musial hit with this thin a handle?" or "Check out this Nellie Fox—no knob!" or "How in the world does Clemente lift this thing?" Eventually, you'd get to the one that felt just right, and for me that was the K55: large barrel, medium handle, 34 inches long, Mickey's name.

We didn't know the weight then, just the length. In Little League, I used a 32-inch bat; in high school, 33 inches; in college, 34 inches; and starting my first year as a pro, 35 inches. Once you turn pro, of course, you learn the exact weight, which is super-important. In the early years of my career, mine weighed 33 ounces. Then, as I got older, weaker, and smarter, I went to 32. (I'm still staggered when I think that Babe Ruth's regular bat weighed 44 ounces—and he sometimes used heavier ones!) Among the guys from my era, Dick Allen carried the heaviest lumber at 40 ounces.

The Louisville Slugger deal I was offered that June day in Reading provided for a season's supply of bats, paid for by the club, with the understanding that someday, if I did well, I'd get my own model. That was it: no signing bonus, no endorsement fee, just free bats. That was the deal almost every other first-year player signed automatically. (Hey, it was Louisville Slugger.)

Well, I took the Adirondack deal. That's right, Adirondack— the bat with the red ring and the words "Big Stick" on the label. The new kid on the block. Why? Because a set of Rawlings Tony Peña golf clubs came with it.

It turned out to be a great move—for Adirondack. I went on to become the first Adirondack-contracted hitter to make the Hall of Fame. That and $4 will get you a tall latte at your local Starbucks. You see, the company took great care over the years to meet all my bat needs, and any related issues, except one. I never got a fee for my endorsement of their bat. Every photo of me hitting, or anything to do with me as a hitter, promoted their product. I have probably given the Big Stick as much exposure as anyone who has gone to the plate over the last thirty-five years, at least until Mark McGwire came along. And all it cost Adirondack was a set of golf clubs.

Back in the day, most hitters bestowed plenty of TLC on their bats. It was essential, or so we felt. Pete Rose was the most scrupulous in that regard, and it obviously paid off—4,256 times. After every game, Pete would sand the marks the ball made on his bat and then clean it with alcohol. He'd look for the good marks—the ones made by line drives—and compare them to the scrapes of the foul balls. I remember doing this myself, with Pete, as a ritual, every day. We also "boned" our bats, which was done by rubbing the barrel firmly with a large animal bone mounted on a two by four. Every clubhouse had one. It was supposed to firm up the grain and prevent splitting.

Your "gamer" was like a valuable piece of jewelry. More than that: your meal ticket. You guarded it with your life. I kept mine, as do all players now, in my locker. Toward the latter part of my career, my bats were locked up in the equipment room. Can you imagine Barry Bonds's bats? They're probably stashed in a vault somewhere and brought to the game by a Brinks truck.

In my day, bats were judged on the width and the strength of the grain. A bat with a knot near the sweet spot was like gold. Of course, there were ways players tried to tinker with the grain, give it a little boost. I mentioned "boning." Once I tried to hollow out the grain with a nail, and fill the lines with pine tar and resin, but that didn't work. Today's maple bats are covered with lacquer with no grain exposed. They don't require, or get, much care. They break easily on a mis-hit, but the hitter just goes to the next one. And they certainly do the job when applied to the ball correctly.

Then there's cork. Hitters of all eras know, no matter what they say, about corked bats. They have to, mostly because it is part of the normal education that comes free of charge during the idle time around the clubhouse. It's accomplished by anchoring the bat in a lathe, drilling out a half-inch-diameter hole down the head of the bat, jamming cork (or some filler) down the hole, and then using wood putty to fill the end so as to make it look normal. This is done to make the bat lighter and to create a springboard effect, as energy is transferred to the ball through the end of the barrel.

With a tip of the hat to notorious bat corkers Norm Cash, Albert Belle, Graig Nettles, and—as recently as 2003—Sammy Sosa, corked bats seldom make it into a game. It's crazy to take a chance like that today, with so much media attention; and anyway, today's bats generate the same corked-like action on their own. That's right. They're so hard and so light that hitters can produce bat speeds far beyond what we could do with our lumber back in my era. You don't have to be a physicist to know that higher bat speed delivers a significant boost in energy to the ball, thereby causing it to travel farther.

Adirondack and Louisville Slugger slugged it out through the 1970s. As the game moved into the 1980s, a couple of new companies sprang up: Mizuno, with their association with Pete Rose, started to import equipment; and a Canadian company, Cooper, introduced a new bat. As of 2005 there were twenty-nine bat manufacturers on the Major League Baseball approved list. That translates into serious competition for player endorsements and market share, which in turn drives bat makers to improve their product. The common goal: harder and lighter.

Today's hitters, almost across the board, use smaller, lighter bats, similar to my college weight and length (34 inches, 32 ounces). My custom bat model, the Adirondack MS20—a near copy of the Mantle K55—was 35 inches long and weighed 33 ounces. Today, it might be used as the weighted bat in the on-deck circle. (By the way, I was flattered to learn from Adirondack that my MS20 model is still in play today; one of the guys who used it, at least for a time, was Chipper Jones.)

Advancements in bat technology have given today's hitters the lightest and hardest bats in baseball history. The reason we see so many more shattered bats is that they're so light. But it's a double-edged sword: small, light bats are vulnerable, but they're also very hard, and they let the pitcher know when he's made a mistake.

Thirty years ago, players swung an ash or hickory bat. Today, ash and hickory still exist, but more and more players are using maple, a denser and harder wood. Barry Bonds set his home run record with a wand made of solid maple called the Sam Bat.

Let me tell you about an experience I had with a Sam Bat. In 2002, I was asked to join a few Phillies alumni for a home run contest before a game at Veterans Stadium. I hadn't swung a bat in maybe five years, and so I was fearful of not hitting a ball out, but I agreed to do it. What were they going to do, option me to Triple A? Anyway, after four or five swings, I found a little home run timing, and *boom!*, the ball started to go out. I couldn't believe how the ball jumped off that bat. All I had to do was center the ball on the bat, get it into the air, and *bye-bye*.

I know, I know—if I'm going to claim that the maple bat propels the ball abnormally long distances, I'd better have proof. Well, the only proof I have is that I hit 548 fair balls over the fences in the major league games, another 300 foul, and probably 10,000 or more in batting practice, and I'm saying I know an unusual, abnormal feeling (for me) when a ball hits a bat. This was one. Have you ever hit a golf ball with a baseball bat? That's the best way I can describe the feeling. If this little exhibition had taken place in 1980, with the equipment of that era but my swing of 2002, maybe one ball would have left the park. There's *no way* that the combination of the maple Sam Bat and the current baseball didn't add a minimum of 10 to 20 feet to the flight of the ball. I hadn't touched a bat in five years, and in ten swings, this stiff fiftysomething old-timer hit four balls over the fence—and in the first deck—at Veterans Stadium.

And I was just getting warmed up.

Knowing this about the dramatic change in bat technology, don't we need to be mindful of this equipment difference when comparing players from earlier eras to those today? The key word here is "mindful." Nobody's suggesting the development of a mathematical formula that would somehow retroactively level the game's statistics over time. But shouldn't we—in the interest of simple fairness—at least acknowledge technological advances in equipment from era to era, as we compare Bonds to Aaron, or A-Rod to Ernie Banks, or Manny Ramirez to Ted Williams?

The strike zone is defined in the rules as the area over home plate between the hollow beneath the kneecap and the midpoint between the belt and shoulders. Home plate is 17 inches wide and 12 inches deep. For a batter who is six feet tall and assumes a "normal" semicrouched batting stance, the vertical dimension of the strike zone is approximately 36 inches. Multiply 36 x 17 x 12 and you have a strike "box" of 7,344 cubic inches. A ball passing through this zone (as the strike box is customarily known) is a strike.

Simple and straightforward, right?

Wrong. Baseball's strike zone is a moving target—literally. Over the past thirty years, it has shrunk steadily, so that now it's about 33 percent smaller than the official definition. That's right: The actual strike zone is about *one-third* smaller than the rulebook strike zone. Lop off a couple of inches at the bottom and 8 to 10 at the top of the zone, and you're taking a huge burden off a hitter's mind: the high hard one. (Hell, if today's strike zone had been in effect for the whole history of the game, the expression "high hard one" might never have made it into the language.) Just imagine standing in against Roger Clemens if umpires gave him that additional couple of thousand cubic inches above the batter's waist that the rulebook says are his by right. The Rocket would *average* 15 Ks a game.

Fact is, the strike zone—or, rather, its identification and inter-pretation by a fallible human being known as the umpire—causes more arguments among men of goodwill than any other subject in sports, if not all mankind. Tennis employs laser technology to monitor the boundaries of the court on serves. Football reduces the chance of human error with instant replay. Basketball has the 24-second clock and light on the back of the backboard. Horse racing uses strategically placed cameras to determine fouls and, in cases of photo finishes, even the outcome. Only baseball embraces the human factor, defers to it, salutes it, and employs it scores of times every game. Nowhere in competitive sports is something so impor-tant to the outcome of a contest so subject to human judgment—and human frailty.

Different umpires have different tendencies, and smart hitters make it their business to know them. We had an umpire named Frank Pulli—great guy, great umpire—who loved to call strikes. He had this short, right-cross punching strike call. If Steve Carlton was pitching, and Pulli had the plate on a getaway day, you were looking at a one-and-a-half-hour game. Frank's motto was, "Make 'em swing the bat." Ed Vargo was just the opposite, a hitter's um-pire. His strike zone, and this is no exaggeration, was the size of a basketball. I loved hitting when Ed had the plate. The important thing was that they were consistent: Pulli a big zone, Vargo a small one—always.

Today's strike zone doesn't extend upward to the mid-point between the shoulders and belt; often it doesn't even extend up-ward to the belt. Around 50 percent of belt-high pitches are called high, even though they're a good 12 inches below the official upper boundary of the strike zone. That's okay, as long as it's consistent. If umpires all of a sudden started calling mid-chest pitches strikes, there would be hell to pay—and ERAs would drop a run.

Knowing that the small strike zone is hard for the normal big league pitcher to hit under game conditions, I'm dumbfounded by hitters who don't seem to understand the advantages available to them.

Take two extreme cases on my former team, Bobby Abreu and Jimmy Rollins. Bobby is very selective at the plate. As a consequence, he gets good hitting counts, walks more than 100 times a season, has a career .303 BA, and forces the pitcher to challenge him. His career on-base percentage is .411. In 2005 he saw more pitches than any other hitters in the majors. Jimmy, on the other hand, can't wait to swing, no matter what the score. He's not as tall as Bobby, and thus has a smaller zone. Even though Jimmy usually hits leadoff, his OBP is .328. Two very good hitters, two very different styles: one who lets the strike zone work for him, another who defines the strike zone as anything he thinks he can reach.

Squeezed by a smaller strike zone, pitchers work away from the bat, relying more on ball movement to get hitters out and way less on challenging hitters in the strike zone than their predecessors did twenty to thirty years ago. For this approach to work, a pitcher needs pinpoint control, and control is the hardest thing to master. The net effect of the smaller strike zone is a big boost in offense. A small strike zone increases the chance of the hitter landing in good hitting counts: 1–0, 2–0, 3–0, 3–1—hello, fastball in the zone. The more you hit in these counts, the higher your production. Just ask Bobby Abreu. So, with pitchers wanting to avoid contact, and umpires squeezing them, why be an aggressive hitter early in an at-bat? Sure, there'll be occasions when it's smart to go up there and let it fly, but the patient hitter, over time, will always be better off.

Another reason for the home run explosion of the last decade or so is crystal clear: shorter power alleys in many of the thirteen new, hitter-friendly ballparks opened for play since Camden Yards made its debut in 1992.

Build it and they will come? Maybe. Build it smaller and those who come will see a whole lot more home runs flying over the fences? Absolutely. Next question?

Okay, okay—not so fast. It's true that major league sluggers have always loved stepping up to the plate in Boston and Chicago, where Fenway's Green Monster and Wrigley's Friendly Confines can turn a slump into a hot streak over the course of a three-game series. And Atlanta–Fulton County Stadium (1965–96, RIP) was known affectionately (and with good reason) as the Launching Pad.

But power hitters in the three decades before the 1990s had to struggle with the other end of the spectrum as well. National Leaguers had the Astrodome (1965–99) in Houston (gigantic in the alleys, plus air-deadening AC); Candlestick, in San Francisco, where the wind ate up home runs; Dodger Stadium, always a pitcher's park, with 385-foot alleys; and all the cookie-cutter, multipurpose stadiums (Shea, the Vet, Riverfront, Three Rivers), which gave pitchers an edge. Over in the American League, big yards in Oakland, Kansas City, Chicago, Detroit, Anaheim, Baltimore, and Toronto kept long fly balls in the house, while Texas and Minnesota were a little more like Atlanta.

A power hitter who plays in a smaller park has an obvious home run advantage. In Fenway, for example, a right-handed hitter who can get a little air under the ball never wants to leave home. Yankee Stadium has a short porch in right that is pure heaven for left-handed pull hitters. Wrigley, of course, favors all hitters. But these older parks are quirky, and small in certain areas, and they've been around long enough for their impact to have been absorbed into historical benchmarks. Wrigley Field, at one end of what we can call the Hitter Friendly–Pitcher Friendly Spectrum, has been around since 1914, so it's not been a major contributing factor to the home run spike in recent times. Wrigley's always been there. I hope it always will be.

The proliferation of new ballparks over the past decade and a half, and their collective impact on baseball's records and history, is quite another matter. They have had a huge impact. In the twenty seasons between 1973 (my first full year in the majors) and the opening of Camden Yards in 1992, the home run rate was .65 per game. From 1993 through 2005, it was 1.04 per game. That's a 60 *percent* jump. Since 1995, when Coors Field came on line, the HR rate is 1.08 per game, 66 percent higher than in my era.

My point should be pretty obvious: The thirteen new ballparks built in the last decade and a half have dramatically inflated home run totals and, in the process, have undermined the baseball record book.

Today, NL hitters get a crack at six "Wrigleys": Minute Maid in Houston, Miller Park in Milwaukee, Great American in Cincinnati, Bank One Ballpark in Phoenix, Citizens Bank in Philadelphia—and, of course, good old Wrigley Field itself in Chicago. (Is the wind blowing out?) And then, as a special bonus for playing in the right era, they get to hit at Coors Field, every modern slugger's field of dreams.

Understand, I'm not degrading today's hitters, much less blaming them. They didn't build the new ballparks. But they know that every fly ball has a chance to leave the yard when they play in them. Additionally, once a power hitter understands and develops a knack for a small-park swing—short and smooth, just center the ball—he can take extreme advantage of the conditions.

What's so wrong with this scenario? Almost nothing—and it's helped return the game to prominence from its early 1990s decline. But there's one big downside: the cheapening effect on individual records and baseball's history, cherished by baseball fans more than in any other sport.

At some point soon, Barry Bonds—708 homers entering the 2006 season—will, if he stays healthy, pass both Babe Ruth (714) and Hank Aaron (755) on the all-time home run list. But keep in mind that if Hank had played in Barry's era instead of 1954–76, the target number Bonds is shooting for would be bigger, *way* bigger.

Let's step back a bit. Let's take my own career homer total—
548—and break it down. Then let's project what it might reasonably have been had *I* played in the Home Run Era, 1990–2005.

Ready?

Okay, I averaged 37 homers a year over my most productive
fourteen seasons (1974–87). Accept that in each of those years I
flied out to the outfield warning track—10 feet short of a home
run—about 50 times, 25 at home and 25 on the road. On the conservative side, 10 of those 25 fly balls at home would be home runs
today, bringing my annual average to 47. Give me another five on
the road, because of at-bats in small parks like Cincinnati, Milwaukee, Denver, Phoenix, and Houston, and the annual average climbs
to 57. Round it down to 50. Still with me?

Let's go back and be conservative again. Scale back and say +10
is the magic number. Still with me? Okay, I'm absolutely comfortable saying I would have hit 10 more home runs per year if I had
played from 1992 through 2005. That's 140 additional home runs.
Using this formula, and throwing my first and last two seasons back
into the mix, I'd have been pushing 700 homers when I finally decided to hang up my spikes.

Project Hank Aaron's career total 755 home runs, which he hit
in twenty-three years at an average of more than 32 per year (32.8,
if you're scoring at home) at 42 per year—10 more homers per season, a realistic figure given today's ballparks. (You have to figure
that, like Bonds and McGwire, Hank would have popped 55–65 a
few times.) That would bring his all-time HR record to 966!

Barry Bonds played four years prior to 1990, so adding 40 to
his current total would put him at 743 entering the 2006 season,
or about four to five more years of solid production away from the
record that Hank would have achieved with my new—and more
realistic—math.

You're looking at me again. It's that "get over it" look. You want me to let go of this whole "it was harder when I played" and "today's players have it easy" attitude, right? Well, it's tough for us old guys to watch the standards change without getting the respect we deserve. It's an ego thing. I ended my career at seventh all-time in home runs; now I'm eleventh, with Junior Griffey nipping at my heels. With normal good health—and the good Lord willing—I'll be alive to see myself drop out of the top 20.

The 500 Home Run Club had fourteen members when I joined in 1986. Next to join was Eddie Murray in 1996. Today the club has twenty members. You realize how many members the club's likely to have by 2020? If I were setting the over-under today, I'd say fifty. Look, the 500 Home Run Club used to be something very special, very exclusive. Qualifying for membership was always at least as much a test of longevity as it was a test of power. To get in, you needed sixteen to twenty seasons of 30 homers a year, when 30 was a highly respected number. Hitting 40–45 virtually locked up an MVP award.

And 50? By the time I retired, that number had been reached seventeen times *in the first nine decades of the twentieth century.* Since 1990, twelve guys have hit 50 or more homers a grand total of twenty times.

Look at it another way. If the current HR boom continues unchecked, then 15 years from now the 700 Club will no longer be remembered as a Christian TV show.

Even so, breaking Hank Aaron's career home run mark, the most celebrated record in all of sports, will require a prodigious combination of talent, effort, and luck over a long career. And when (not if) it is broken—by Barry Bonds, or Albert Pujols, or Adam Dunn, or a first-round draft pick this spring who'll snap up a $2 million signing bonus—a giant floodlight of attention will be beamed on changes in the game since 1990 that helped make it happen.

That light will fall on the ball (of course) . . . the bat . . . the strike zone . . . new parks . . . better training . . . and, yes, steroids.

But on that fine summer day when somebody finally swats number 756, keep in mind that Hank Aaron, had he played in the Boom-Boom Years, would still be a couple hundred dingers ahead of the pack.

11 Deck the Hall

Every baseball fan needs to make one trip to Cooperstown. Nothing will make you appreciate our game more than a slow, meandering walk through the Hall of Fame—and the picture-postcard town that houses it. For a true baseball fan, the little city of Cooperstown is hallowed ground. You can almost smell the hot dogs, beer, and pine tar in the air. Everything about it exudes baseball. The greatest honor in all of sports—okay, I'm prejudiced—is election into the National Baseball Hall of Fame. Sure, other sports have their halls, but none can match the history and tradition and roots in America of the one in Cooperstown.

What does the Hall of Fame mean to baseball? Here's how Jane Forbes Clark, the Hall's chairman, explained it in the foreword of the book *Baseball as America:*

> The National Baseball Hall of Fame has the unique responsibility of preserving baseball's rich history and honoring its

greatest heroes. As the institutional and spiritual home of The Game, we have an even greater responsibility to examine the deeper significance of baseball and reveal its enduring relevance to this great country and all Americans. The artifacts and the legacies that are in our safekeeping tell the story of a people brought together by a set of shared values and aspirations.

In that passage, it's not the message that catches my eye so much as the capitalization of the T and G in the words "The Game." In Cooperstown, baseball is the only game in town. In the shops, in the restaurants, along the streets, in the surrounding country, it's baseball.

For those who have never been there, imagine yourself on a hillside in upstate New York, overlooking a green valley, with a beautiful blue lake at the bottom. That lake is nine miles long and one mile wide, and 200 feet deep in the middle. It's called Otsego, an Indian word meaning "clear, deep water." On the end closest to you is a quaint little town of 2,032 residents, founded in 1786 and named after James William Cooper, a judge, member of Congress, and land speculator. (And the father of James Fenimore Cooper, the first great American novelist.) It almost looks like a model train village, with a rainbow of different-colored little buildings framed in century-old trees and surrounded by green hillsides. There are even a few of the stone houses Judge Cooper built 225 years ago. In the little town, there is one stoplight, one supermarket, one pharmacy, a couple of restaurants, a couple of bars, no theaters.

Ah, but there are four museums: the Farmers' Museum, devoted to the region's agricultural past; the Fenimore Art Museum, featuring a highly regarded collection of North American folk art and North American Indian art; the Heroes of Baseball Wax Museum, a single-focus version of Madame Tussaud's, complete with a virtual reality batting cage, three floors of baseball memorabilia, and a Baseball Bloopers Theatre (score it E-5); and, of course, a museum visited by 350,000 people a year (more than 13 million since it opened in 1939), the granddaddy of them all—the National Baseball Hall of Fame.

Like a vast treasure chest full of gold and precious jewels, the Hall houses the cherished relics of baseball's past: 165,000 artifacts, including more than 6,000 balls, 1,800 bats, 450 gloves, 600 hats, 850 jerseys—and 260 plaques commemorating the exploits of the most fortunate men in sports history.

One weekend a year in late July, Cooperstown comes alive as the Hall opens its doors to welcome new recipients of the greatest honor a baseball player can achieve. They call it Induction Weekend. Fans from across the country flock to the little city, on narrow, meandering roads, through forests and over mountains, through small rural towns, just to be there as the latest inductees are enshrined. They come as baseball families, with kids whose father wants to educate them about the old days, when he was their age—and before.

A trip to Cooperstown becomes "Dad's Show and Tell" weekend. "Hey, son, here's a glove used in 1926 with only three fingers. Can you believe they could catch a ball with that?" And "Look at the size of this bat Babe Ruth used!" "Babe Ruth? Who's he?" "Son, he was the Barry Bonds of baseball seventy years ago. He played before I was born." "Boy, he really is an old-timer."

On and on the education continues, generation after generation, fathers and sons and baseball.

On Induction Weekend 1995, it was my turn. After waiting the necessary five years after my retirement, I received 444 votes out of a possible 460 on the first ballot—what in the world were those 16 guys thinking of, anyway?—and got the call. That year the Veterans Committee voted in my friend Richie Ashburn, who joined me in what was to be a weekend never to forget. It's hard to describe the feeling you get in becoming a member. It's being recognized as one of the greatest players ever. It's becoming friends with the greatest. You are in the same fraternity as Babe Ruth, Ty Cobb, Lou Gehrig, Ted Williams, Jackie Robinson, and the game's other great legendary figures. People around the game look at you and refer to you with respect that comes only with membership.

I have no idea how it happened. I just faced my challenges, set my goals high, kept getting up after being knocked down, and added it up at the end. I never gave the Hall a thought until Pete Rose called me a Hall of Famer one day in the early 1980s. Even then I was reluctant to acknowledge such a comment. I might have had a few great years, but the test of staying at the high level of performance over a long time still remained. That's the equalizer, the longevity. Few Hall of Fame players had careers that lasted less than fifteen years: Sandy Koufax is the most notable exception. It's a career survival test, in a game that spans three-fourths of a year, from spring training through the World Series. I played in 2,404 major league games—sounds like a lot, but that's an average Hall of Fame total.

A Hall of Famer is also a guy who defined his position over that time. He didn't just hang on with decent stats; he led the league, won Gold Gloves and MVP awards, and played in postseason games. Less than 1 percent of those who have played in the major leagues ever get HOF consideration. As I said, it's the highest honor I can imagine. Sometimes I need to pinch myself to make sure I'm not dreaming.

If you want to engage a fellow baseball fan in a spirited conversation, just mention the Hall of Fame. There's no subject that runs a close second. Who's going in, who's in but doesn't belong there, who's not in but should be in . . . on and on, until the game's called on account of darkness.

Be careful about raising the subject with me, though, because I believe the selection process is fundamentally flawed by politics and personal bias, and I'm liable to unload on you. Like right now.

But first, an explanation of how it works:

A player with a minimum of 10 years of major league service becomes eligible for election to the Hall of Fame five years after his retirement. His name goes on a ballot of eligible players that is submitted annually in December to the membership of the Baseball Writers Association of America (BBWAA). To be elected to the Hall of Fame, he must receive 75 percent of the votes of the BBWAA. If he receives less than 75 percent, he remains on the ballot for up to fifteen years, provided he receives at least 5 percent of the total votes cast in the preceding year. If he hasn't received the requisite 75 percent of the votes needed for election after the maximum 15 years, he's bound over for consideration by the Veterans Committee, which consists of living Hall of Fame members and winners of the Ford Frick Award (broadcasters) and the J. Taylor Spink Award (sportswriters). The Veterans Committee is empowered to enshrine a player rejected by the voters during his initial 15 years of eligibility.

My problem is that politics and personal bias play too large a role in both cases, especially the voting by the baseball writers.

The year I was elected, 1994, there were 460 voting members of the BBWAA. I received 444 votes; 16 writers didn't vote for me on the first ballot. Now, some baseball writers just don't believe anyone should get in on the first ballot. Others don't take their vote seriously and blow it off. And a few—here's where the politics kicks in—have personal issues with a player. Look, I don't mind baseball writers having personal feelings about players. Hell, I have personal feelings about writers. But when they let personal feelings unrelated to on-field performance influence their votes for the Hall of Fame, I do have a problem. A big problem.

In my case, one Philadelphia writer withheld his vote as pay-back. He and I had verbal differences of opinion over the years, and he used the power of his vote to flex his muscles. He was unable to look past our personal issues, and he figured his one chance to stick it to me for good was through his vote.

(The other fifteen? I'm still trying to track them down.)

Think my case was an isolated occurrence? Think again. Eddie Murray (3,255 hits, 504 home runs) was deemed Hall-worthy by only 85 percent of the voters because of a career-long strained rela-tionship with the media. (The other 15 percent didn't think Eddie deserved to be in the Hall of Fame? That, my friends, is bullshit.) Jim Rice got 64.8 percent of the vote in the balloting for the Class of 2006; had he gotten along better with the press, he'd be in already. (He has three more chances.) Gary Carter, the polar opposite of Rice in terms of his relations with the writers, was inducted in 2003—his sixth year of eligibility.

The voting writers lobby for and against players. Players on the bubble who were great interviews, were accessible, and seemed to respect the media get the benefit of the doubt. Those with testy relations with the press get the opposite. It's human nature, I guess. If I were a voter and a player disrespected me and my job, why shouldn't I punish him at voting time? The way it's set up, the se-lection process allows the BBWAA writer to do just that—and that's why I think it's fundamentally flawed.

I feel election to the Hall of Fame is such a high honor that politics and personal bias should have no place in the process.

That said, I believe deciding who enters the Hall of Fame has been a responsibility that most members of the BBWAA have discharged fairly and with respect. And I don't see the election process changing, because it's served baseball reasonably well over the years. But it is my opinion that the Hall's exclusivity could be preserved better under another process. In my proposed system, the original vote would not be the deciding vote; it would only qualify a player to be reviewed by a smaller blue-ribbon committee with final authority. This would be a committee of distinguished, respected senior writers nominated and elected by their peers. This panel would function much like a jury, weighing the evidence before returning its verdict. I feel this would flush out the politics and the personal bias and allow a player's qualifications to be judged solely on their merits.

One other thing: Even though the annual Hall of Fame vote gives baseball a midwinter public relations boost and Induction Weekend is a midsummer bonanza for Cooperstown, nowhere is it written that at least one player must be voted in every year. If the Hall of Fame is to be reserved for only the game's best, then there will be years when no player merits induction. That's okay. In fact, it's necessary if the Hall's to remain what it's always been—a sacred place.

By the way, it's not surprising that since 2003, when it was revamped to include living Hall of Famers, the Veterans Committee has selected no player for admission to the Hall. Score one for human nature: Members of a club are always looking for ways to make their club more exclusive.

Voters have a monumental task ahead of them over the next ten years, and maybe beyond. Several prominent stars with HOF credentials, all of whom have been associated with steroid use, will become eligible for the Hall of Fame. As of November 2005, none of these men—with the major exception of Rafael Palmeiro—has tested positive for steroids or admitted to steroid use. The only "evidence" is leaked testimony and claims of ignorance. That could change, with hard evidence replacing rumor, but if it doesn't, decisions will be easy.

Mark McGwire retired from baseball after the 2001 season with

583 career home runs and 1,414 RBI in 1,874 games over sixteen seasons; one Most Valuable Player award; one World Series ring; and the popular credit, which he shared with Sammy Sosa, for having saved baseball in the 1990s. His name will be on the Hall of Fame ballot in December 2006. Should he be voted in by the 460+ electors?

The question extends beyond Big Mac, of course. It will be repeated down the road when other great sluggers of the Steroid Era—Palmeiro, Sammy Sosa, Barry Bonds—become eligible. How should the HOF electors react when they see those names and others from the Steroid Era on the ballot?

If I were a sportswriter with a vote right now, here is what I would know as fact. Steroids allow muscles to recover faster, so an athlete can work out longer and harder, permitting him to build more muscle mass faster. More mass = more strength. More strength = more bat speed. More bat speed = more power. That's it. That's what I know steroids do. But steroids don't give a player the will to get up and go to the gym at 6 A.M. or to spend an hour in the weight room after games. He still has to push himself. And steroids don't enable him to hit to all fields or cut down on his strikeouts.

Steroids = Power. Period.

But if I used steroids, kept my normal workout routine, and could see in the mirror that my body was changing, wouldn't I be more inclined to accommodate my body, as it told me to push harder because my muscles can take more? Wouldn't that psychological boost push me to the gym more often for longer workouts? Wouldn't I enjoy the new me, once a 180-pound gap hitter with occasional power, now an intimidating 220-pound slugger with big power to all fields? The fly ball to right center that used to be caught on the warning track now goes into the seats. Hitting that fly ball is easy, and now with the added muscle mass, it's a double or a home run. Won't pitchers view me as different, more threatening? Hell, yes.

So maybe using steroids can do more than add a few dingers to one's résumé. If you buy this scenario, you might also buy the notion that all the players in question who made big splashes in the Steroid Era—those who tested positive, plus those whose size and offensive output shrank visibly and significantly in the 2005 season—must have become different people and had an unfair advantage during their alleged steroid use period. If you believe that, the final test would be an additional season or two. Player A might have shrunk 30 pounds and his home run total might have dropped by 20 in 2005, but that's only one season. His numbers may bounce back to pre-2005 levels in 2006 or 2007 and shoot down this theory. But if Player A never returns to his inflated year numbers, then one would logically suspect that steroids had been a distinct advantage for him.

If steroids were legal without a prescription, and available equally to all players, there would be no issue. But they're not. They're illegal without a prescription, so the illegality becomes the centerpiece of the problem. If a player is tested and found to have an illegal substance in his body, I find it hard to believe he would qualify for the Hall of Fame.

That brings us back to Big Mac. It's December 2006. Hall of Fame ballots are being distributed. If I had a vote, how would I cast it?

Mark McGwire in the Hall of Fame: yes or no?

Okay, here's what I know about Mark McGwire right now. I know he used androstenedione, a legal substance, because he admitted he did. I also know he was never tested for steroids, because baseball had no drug policy of consequence when he was an active player. I know Jose Canseco said he taught Mark how to inject himself with steroids, but that's unconfirmed hearsay from an unreliable accuser. I know Mark used evasive, nonresponsive language under oath in responding to questions before Congress about steroid use—in effect, invoking the Fifth Amendment's protection against self-incrimination, as was his constitutional right to do. And I know he has impeccable Hall of Fame credentials that would, under normal circumstances, make him a first-ballot Hall of Famer.

So, based on what I know, and disregarding what I might suspect based on unconfirmed speculation and rumor, I would vote yes—bring Mark McGwire into the Hall of Fame.

What about Palmeiro? His career stats mark him as a shoo-in first-ballot Hall of Famer when he becomes eligible five years from now. Will he be voted in? Certainly not if he were on the ballot this year. And probably not when he becomes eligible in 2010, unless he manages somehow to shed credible new light on his having tested positive for steroid use. More likely, he will never be honored for 3,000–500, but will always be remembered for "Never. Period."

And what about the others? Barry Bonds? Sammy Sosa?

I say we don't condemn anybody based on speculation and rumor.

Back in the 1990s, when steroids began to pollute the game, players didn't have a crystal ball. Do you think a player back then would have used, knowing that all of his accomplishments, including a possible Hall of Fame election, would be questioned? Probably not. Had a rigorous testing program been in place, would anybody have used? Absolutely not. But life is a long series of decisions that shape us as people, and you have to live with them. The players who used steroids and didn't get caught are lucky. The ones who got caught—and those who still may get caught—have to live with the consequences.

Those consequences are mixed. The player who used illegal steroids to enhance his performance undoubtedly played at levels he would not otherwise have reached. In the Boom-Boom Years, that translated into more money, a lot more money. The flip side is that he may not make the Hall of Fame, may have lost the respect of baseball fans, and may find his accomplishments discredited. But he's filthy rich, financially set for life.

Was it worth it?

• • •

As a boy I collected baseball cards. We all did. They came in a pack of five with that rectangular piece of strange-tasting bubble-gum. Getting a Hall of Famer in the pack was sweet, but getting a Mantle, a Williams, a Mays, a Jackie Robinson, a Musial, or any other current player obviously destined for Cooperstown was even sweeter. They were my guys, my Hall of Famers to-be. Probably the neatest thing about being in the Hall for me is that those guys are now my friends. I get to rub shoulders with players I once thought were gods, players whose cards I had once cherished.

(Old song, slightly different verse: Yes, my mom finally got rid of my cards, but at least she sold them in a charity auction.)

My plaque hangs in the same room as those of my heroes. They sat behind me as I delivered my acceptance speech, as I now sit behind new members when they give theirs. I belong to a special family of men. I have a legacy that will forever be on display for all to see. My grandchildren's kids will be able to go to Cooperstown and see my plaque and my display.

What could be a greater honor? Would I have done anything, no matter what the financial rewards might have been, to risk not receiving it?

My answer, based on crystal-clear 20/20 hindsight, is no.

No. Had I played in the Steroid Era, and had I thought that using steroids might in any way jeopardize my being inducted into the Hall of Fame, I would not have hesitated in reaching my decision.

No.

12   What About Pete?

Every time I'm around a group of people and the talk turns to base-ball, sooner or later—and usually sooner—someone asks The Ques-tion: Do you think Pete Rose should be in the Hall of Fame?

I'll tell you my thoughts on that in a minute, but first let me give you a little deep background, so you'll understand where I'm coming from.

Pete was banned from baseball by Commissioner Bart Giamatti on August 24, 1989. A written agreement prepared by the Com-missioner's Office spelled out the details of the ban. It stated that if Pete accepted this decision, based on the findings of a six-month-long investigation headed by John Dowd that Rose had indeed placed bets on baseball games while managing the Reds, then the report would not be made public and the investigation would ter-minate. Basically, no official finding would be released saying that Rose bet on baseball games if Pete agreed to disappear quietly. The agreement further stated he could apply for reinstatement after one year. Pete agreed to these terms and signed the document.

Two very important things then happened: Commissioner Giamatti died of a massive heart attack eight days later; and Pete began
contending, emphatically and publicly, that he had never bet on
baseball, and that the evidence against him came from witnesses
looking to strike plea bargains. A year later, Pete attempted to apply for reinstatement, but was not permitted to do so by the new
commissioner, Fay Vincent. That's where things have stood ever
since: Pete Rose, the all-time hits leader, one of the greatest players
who ever lived, banned from baseball.

Pete's banishment has weighed very heavily on him and his
family. He has had immense financial problems triggered by a free-
fall drop in income as a result of the ban. He has had major problems with the IRS. And he has had to carry a crippling burden of
guilt. Pete's life was baseball, and to be forbidden to be involved
with any aspect of it was for him the equivalent of pure torture.

Over the last decade and a half, it's true, he has developed a
strong, numerous, and highly vocal support base, made up in part
of fans who believed Pete when he said he didn't bet on the game,
and in perhaps greater part of fans who saw him as baseball's "bad
boy" and were prepared to forgive and forget.

Through all this, Pete was a thorn in the side of Vincent's suc-
cessor, Commissioner Bud Selig. Whenever Pete and Mr. Selig
would turn up at the same event, such as the All Century Team
celebration at the All-Star Game in Atlanta in 1999 or the 100
Greatest World Series Moments festivity in San Francisco in 2002,
Rose would get standing ovations and Mr. Selig would hear a cho-
rus of boos.

All this time, Pete chose to live with his lie; evidently that burden was easier to bear than the fallout from any confession of truth
he might make. That came to an end shortly following the San Francisco World Series appearance when former teammate Joe Morgan
told Pete he would go to bat for him, but only if Pete came forward

and told the truth. This meant one of the game's most respected Hall of Famers would stand behind him if Pete would lay himself at the mercy of the commissioner and the public and confess.

Would the truth set Pete Rose free?

Enter yours truly. Following the exchange in San Francisco between Pete and his old Big Red Machine teammate, and Mr. Selig's subsequent agreement to meet with Pete, I got a call from the Commissioner's Office. Mr. Selig, who knew I was a friend and supporter of Pete, asked me to serve as a liaison between him and Pete. This was a surprise. Mr. Selig and I were acquaintances, but we'd had little if any history as business associates. I was honored to be asked to participate, and thought this would be a chance to help Pete get right with baseball. You see, like just about everybody who knew Pete, I wanted to believe his story, and I always gave him the benefit of the doubt publicly. But knowing Pete's penchant for gambling and his habit of hanging out with sleazy people, it wasn't hard for me to see the other side as a potential reality.

But before I could go to bat for Pete, I had to know that he was going to be totally honest and forthright with me regarding baseball and gambling. I would not put my own reputation in jeopardy in support of anything shady or duplicitous, as we were moving headlong into a national media explosion, and I would be smack in the middle. I also believed Pete needed the help of a close friend, someone he respected, someone who wanted only the best for him, someone who wasn't looking to take advantage of him.

Maybe most important, I believed Pete to have a gigantic heart, always willing to give of himself to those around him. I knew he had always been lacking, mostly of his own doing, a personal life of love and friendship. I thought this might put him in a more human light, not only with the commissioner and with fans, but with his family. Pete would be in a position totally unfamiliar to him, one over which he had no control, no wiggle room, no influence, no bargaining power, and no celebrity power to draw on. It would be Pete Rose, naked to the baseball world, telling the plain if painful truth.

I thought that if Pete was honest and expressed genuine remorse, it couldn't fail. Pete Rose opens his heart, confesses, and asks for forgiveness. He agrees to speak out against gambling, does community service, and dedicates his life to promoting a clean game. How many times had baseball let its druggie bad boys off after confessions of guilt? It was, and is, human nature to forgive, and baseball would forgive Pete, accept him back, and applaud the commissioner for his effort.

It was a win/win opportunity for all concerned.

The meeting was set for November 25, 2002, three days before Thanksgiving, in Milwaukee. That morning, I met Pete and Warren Greene, his adviser, for breakfast. Pete and I sat across from each other. I looked him in the eye and said, "Are you ready for this"? He smiled, and said "Herbie"—for some reason, he's always called me "Herbie"—"I can't go on any longer." He seemed ready to face the music. But I sensed that he still saw this as something he could control, and would attempt to do so if given half a chance. I added nothing more, just filed that thought away, and we headed to meet with Mr. Selig.

Arriving by limo, we were escorted up a private elevator by a security guard to baseball's highest office. An entire floor overlooking the city and Lake Michigan, devoted to the Commissioner of Baseball and his staff. The carpeting was a red baseball design, very tasteful. The walls were adorned with baseball art and a few nice collectibles. Everything was plush and tasteful, absolutely first class.

Bud—I'll call him Bud from here on; I think he'd prefer that—was of course on the phone, where he spends a good part of the day, so we were directed into the conference room. There Bob DuPuy,

the president of MLB and Bud's top assistant, greeted us with coffee. The four of us chatted about the latest in sports, easy to do
anytime Pete's around.

After a few minutes, Bud was ready for us, at which time we
gathered in his office. The commissioner sat behind his desk,
framed by a panoramic view of Lake Michigan. It was a clear, sunny
fall day. Pete sat to my left, Warren Greene to my right, and Bob
DuPuy sat next to Warren.

The initial part of the meeting was casual and nonconfronta-
tional, with Bud and Pete exchanging views on current sports news,
and DuPuy updating the group on his initial meeting with us in
Florida. I felt good about the way things seemed to be going, as Bud
exchanged glances with me and looked for my reaction to certain
points. I chimed in when we discussed the issue of a probationary
period, supporting an agreement that would have Pete report to the
commissioner regularly on his state of affairs, during which time
Pete would not be prohibited from pursuing work in the game. Our
position was that Pete had served his time and shouldn't be offered
only a partial reinstatement. Make him prove his rehabilitation is
working, and make sure he understands his reinstatement can be
revoked, but don't limit his opportunities. Everyone seemed on the
same page. We touched on a likely itinerary for Pete over the next
couple of months.

And then we moved to the real reason for the visit: Pete's confession to Bud.

After discussing plans for Pete's reinstatement, Bud asked to
speak with Pete alone. That was our cue to move back to the conference room. Now, I wasn't in Bud's office, and I didn't hear an actual word of the "official" confession—nobody did, except Bud. But
I know for a fact that Pete Rose admitted he bet on the Reds while
he was manager, just as he had been accused of doing in 1989.

Bud Selig told me so.

• • •

Except on a baseball field, Pete Rose is not an outwardly emotional man, never has been, probably never will be. Any documentary you've seen or book you've read about Pete has told you he's like his father: tough, thick-skinned, street-smart. As his career blossomed, then flowered into one of the greatest ever, Pete got special treatment from people around him—and grew to expect it. I sensed he thought he could still somehow find an angle to save face. He'd tell Bud the truth, they'd shake hands, set a press release date, case closed.

Bud wanted more. Pete's confession lacked one major thing in Bud's mind: remorse. If it were me, and I had lived with that cancer in my brain for fourteen years, constantly digging a deeper hole for myself, I'd have sobbed on my knees at the feet of the commissioner, begging for forgiveness. I'd have thrown myself on the mercy of the one man who could restore my standing in the only world where I felt I belonged: baseball.

Not Pete. He said his piece. He was honest. But at the same time, he was still looking for an angle, not asking for one, but expecting to find one hidden somewhere. Again, I wasn't there, but I spoke to Bud later, and he told me he got the confession he had expected, but not the expression of genuine remorse he had hoped for. As it would turn out, that missing expression of remorse was more than "hoped for." It was required.

At the time, though, the meeting seemed to be a success. Over lunch, we talked some more about the initial press release, the national press conference, and the outline of the terms of the agreement, all of which would be followed up on in detail by Bob DuPuy in future meetings. Pete, Warren, and I were very satisfied by Bud's preliminary reaction as we left for the airport. We thought a positive response from the commissioner was a lock. We thought Pete was going to be accepted back by baseball. We thought he was going to be allowed to come home.

Three years later, Pete's still waiting to hear from Bud.

Rose never got that positive response. He's gotten *no* response. His case has been in limbo, with no action or communication whatsoever over the last three years. Why? I believe there are several reasons. First, I believe Bud still feels a sense of obligation to the family of Bart Giamatti. Reinstating Pete might have sent a message that Bud had caved in on this important issue, an issue that some say contributed to Mr. Giamatti's untimely death. Second, Bud has friends in high places—the highest of places, the Hall of Fame, where membership is lopsided against ever allowing Pete Rose a chance to enter. Bud has been deeply influenced by the opposition of most Hall of Famers to Pete's reinstatement. Third, I think Bud was truly disappointed in the lack of remorse shown by Pete at the 2002 meeting.

About a year after the Milwaukee meeting, I phoned Bud to ask what was holding up his decision on Pete's reinstatement. Bud confided that he didn't think Pete understood the gravity of this commitment. Bud had heard rumors of Pete showing up at the racetrack in L.A., of his being seen at casinos in Las Vegas, and of his negotiating with the IRS on delinquent tax issues. All of these things were manageable, and not inherently serious, unless you had just confessed to the Commissioner of Baseball that you had lied about betting on the game for fourteen years, that you wanted to change your lifestyle, and that you wanted to be forgiven.

So I promised Bud I'd meet with Pete in private and try to determine for myself whether Pete, in his heart, truly knew what he was faced with, what his responsibilities were, and what he'd have to do to secure the goodwill and cooperation of the Commissioner of Baseball. That meeting took place in the late fall of 2003 in Cincinnati, where I sat alone with Pete, face to face, and confronted him with what I felt he had to do.

"Pete, I need to know, and I need you to be straight with me:

Are you willing to change your lifestyle, get help for the gambling, and in general walk the straight and narrow if you're reinstated?"

Pete said he was. He said he understood there was no shortcut, no wiggle room, no angle. He said he would become a new man. He said he'd get professional help for the gambling, stay away from casinos, and become a model spokesman for baseball.

Once again, I was convinced Pete was being straight with me, and would do whatever was asked of him by baseball. I relayed this to Bud, reminded him how long Pete had been waiting for a decision, assured him that Pete was willing to cooperate fully, and asked if he could give Pete something soon, one way or the other.

Nothing happened—until January 2004, when a bombshell exploded.

The fuse had been lit eleven months earlier, in February 2003— less than three months after the Milwaukee meeting with the commissioner—when Pete signed a contract with Rodale Books for an advance against royalties of nearly seven figures to write a book.

Pete needed money. He saw the book as a big financial opportunity. The book sales, a possible movie deal, increased fees for public appearances at events, maybe a sequel—who knows, but this was going to be the truth about a story that had had the country guessing for years, so the financial benefits looked huge. Pete still had a costly lifestyle, and his income from memorabilia shows wasn't exactly paying the bills.

Now, you don't get an advance of nearly a million bucks for just any book. Certainly not a memoir of the glory days of the Big Red Machine, or a treatise on hitting, and especially not a rehash of what Pete had been saying over and over for fourteen years— namely, that he had never, ever bet on baseball games, period. No publisher was going to pay that kind of money for anything short of a tell-all, come-clean confession that I, Pete Rose, *did* bet on baseball games while I was a manager in the major leagues.

Baseball books come out in bunches the first two months of every year. Christmas is over, the bowl games have come and gone, and box score–starved baseball fans scan the sports page anxiously every day for those magic words, "Pitchers and catchers report February 15." Mostly, they hit the bookstores in early February, shortly after the Super Bowl. (That's when you picked up this one, right?) Sometimes, though, a baseball book with a special buzz generated by advance reading copies distributed to the media will jump out ahead of the pack. That's what happened to Pete Rose's My *Prison Without Bars*.

Pete's book hit the world on Sunday, January 4, 2004. And I do mean *hit*.

It wasn't supposed to happen when it did or the way it did. Pete had a media deal with ABC and *Sports Illustrated*. He was to appear, exclusively, on ABC's *Primetime* with Charlie Gibson on the Thursday night of release week, with a tease on Thursday morning's *Good Morning America*. This *Primetime* segment had been taped a month earlier, with confidentiality agreements signed by all attending. *Sports Illustrated* was the exclusive outlet for book excerpts. *My Prison Without Bars* was scheduled to be at bookstores on Friday, January 9.

The preceding Sunday night—January 4—a friend of Pete's in Cincinnati got dogged by a reporter from the local NBC affiliate into saying, on camera, that Pete admitted to betting on baseball in his upcoming book.

Now, believe me, this was no small thing. This was major national news, information baseball fans all over the country had wanted to hear for more than a decade, delivered by a casual friend of Pete's whose ego apparently couldn't wait to blab to a local Cincinnati reporter. The story exploded on the wires immediately and blew the carefully orchestrated ABC/*Sports Illustrated* plan clean out of the water.

ABC, on learning that NBC had scooped "their" story, had to

move—and fast. Pete pleaded with them to wait and stick with the
original deal, but they really had no choice. Meanwhile, *SI* prepared
to jam their excerpt into the magazine a week ahead of schedule.
ABC rushed Pete to New York on Monday, January 5 for the whirl-
wind cycle of appearances on all their sports and news shows they
had originally booked for Friday. On them, Pete confessed that he
had bet on baseball games as manager of the Reds, but never against
the Reds, and he could no longer live with the secret.

All media hell broke loose. ESPN—like ABC, owned by the
Walt Disney Company—went bananas. TV and sports talk radio
latched on to the story like it was free money, every sports page in every newspaper in the country gave it banner treatment for days, and
bookstores clamored to get books from warehouses into their front-
of-the-store tables reserved for the hottest of the hot new titles.

Great timing, if you're Rodale Books. Publishers can't buy pub-
licity like this.

Horrible timing, if you're Pete Rose, and you're trying to persuade the commissioner to let you back into baseball. Why? Because *My Prison Without Bars* became the number one sports story
in the land the day before the 2004 Hall of Fame inductees, Paul
Molitor and Dennis Eckersley, showed up in New York for *their*
press conference, an annual rite that marks the unofficial start of
each new baseball season.

No one knew Molitor and Eck were alive that week. To the
sports media, and thus to baseball fans, there was only one baseball
story, the guy they used to call Charlie Hustle.

Keep in mind that fourteen months earlier, Pete had confessed
to Bud Selig in a top-secret meeting, and then he'd backed off, shut
up, and waited. And waited. Only now, at precisely the time of year
when baseball nudges football aside for a minute to salute its finest,
Pete's story—a story that baseball sees as a permanent blemish on
the game—was all anyone was talking about.

The bottom line: The timing looked sleazy, *really* sleazy. Pete came under immediate fire for having choreographed the whole thing, for upstaging Molitor and Eckersley, for trying to prove that his confession was bigger than any other news in sports, including the Hall of Fame announcement. Now, in the hundreds of media interviews he did that week, Pete had the double burden of both confessing to gambling on baseball and doing damage control for confessing it on the eve of one of baseball's cherished moments. And Pete's never been very good at damage control.

I don't blame Pete for this. The official release date for *My Prison Without Bars* was January 9, 2004. The excerpt in *Sports Illustrated* was originally scheduled to coincide with the book's release date. Pete had absolutely no control over the jump-start.

I don't blame Rodale Books. Their job is to move product, and Pete's book has racked up over 100,000 copies sold to date.

I don't blame *Sports Illustrated*. The excerpt that they'd paid good money for would have been worthless if they'd held it another week.

I don't blame the networks. They were just doing their job.

I do blame Pete's goofball friend in Cincinnati for shooting off his mouth. Some friend.

Pete's popularity with his legions of fans, dealt a serious blow by his admissions, suffered as well from subsequent criticism of "his" timing. Worse still, the Commissioner, who counts Paul Molitor as a close personal friend, now had another reason to relegate Pete Rose's application to the round file. Spokesmen for the Commissioner's Office were noncommittal about the outburst surrounding Pete's book, saying only that they were still working on the Rose case. They could have softened the blow for Pete by emphasizing that he did admit everything to the commissioner fourteen months earlier. And the public relations fiasco could have been prevented altogether had the commissioner acted in some way during this period. But nothing was done to counter the anti-Pete backlash.

Personally, I think the timing and manner of the book's release, given that it overshadowed the New York Hall of Fame press conference, sealed Pete's fate. For some reason, the commissioner wants to keep Pete on permanent hold. Pete only wants a verdict, one way or another: Yes, we want you back; or No, it's not going to happen.

What about Pete? He's a beaten man. He understands he'll probably never be inducted into the Hall of Fame. He understands that many—perhaps most—of his contemporaries in the Hall oppose his admission. He understands he'll almost certainly never be allowed to return to baseball in any capacity. Support his admission to the Hall of Fame or not, but have empathy for the man, if not for all his off-the-field actions.

What about me?

Do I think Pete Rose should be in the Hall of Fame?

You can probably guess where I stand. To me, Pete Rose and baseball are inseparable. His baseball story is one of the greatest chapters in the game's history. I'd prefer a happy ending, and I haven't given up hope that we'll have one. But no matter how it ends, his story is a vital legacy for all baseball fans, especially young ones who never enjoyed the privilege of seeing him play.

Pete bet on baseball. He bet on his own team to win. Against baseball law? Absolutely. So heinous a crime that it must never be forgiven? Not in my book. Had Pete thrown games, or ever played to lose, we wouldn't be having a conversation. *But Peter Edward Rose Sr. never played to lose at anything.* He played in more winning games than any player in history. He was a winner. What he did was bad. But not bad enough to banish him from baseball forever.

That said, I don't think Pete should be allowed to manage in the major leagues. He committed his offense against the game while he was a manager; not being able to return to such a position would be a fair penalty. Otherwise, Pete should be reinstated, placed on the Hall of Fame ballot for consideration by the Veterans Committee, and be allowed to return to the good graces of the game to which he gave so much. He should be used to counsel current players on the dangers of gambling, much as Don Newcombe did at one time with alcoholism. He should be allowed to take advantage of baseball's licensing opportunities. Pete could be a great asset to the game again. Ignoring that fact is just plain ridiculous.

Pete Rose has served his time, and then some: Let's bring him back.

As for the Hall of Fame, let him meet with the current members, let him ask for their forgiveness, and let them decide.

Going in, I know of one yes vote.

Mine.

POSTSCRIPT

The memory will be with me forever. I'm ten years old. I'm sitting with my grandmother in her room, staring at the poster of Pete Rose that hangs on the back of her bedroom door, as she's trying to make my baseball uniform fit just like Pete's. Life was so simple then.

13 Summer School

Since my retirement in 1989, I've been haunted by a single baseball question: What would it be like to manage in the major leagues?

Life has pulled me in several different directions over that period, none of them along a path that would yield an answer to that question. But something inside has always told me—and still does—that I have what it takes to be a good big league manager. I know how to play baseball to win—that's a given—and I have the leadership qualities to motivate twenty-five young individuals to put all personal priorities aside and play as a team.

The question isn't whether I have what it takes but how much I'm willing to give.

I have a fantastic life. I'm hesitant to pull up the roots I've put down in Florida, curtail the freedom I currently have to pursue just about anything I want to do, and give myself over 100 percent to the demanding, high-pressure, high-profile, energy-draining life of a big league manager. Not only that, but I'm not eager to become a slave once again to room service, Spectra-Vision, and hotel bars.

Managing a major league baseball team is a time-sucking grind. From mid-February (when pitchers and catchers report) to Opening Day to the final out of the World Series (if you're lucky), it's a 24/7 deal. Maybe you can piece together a month off in the winter, but most of your "off-season" is spent on the job: taking part in organizational meetings, going to MLB's winter meetings, scouting winter ball leagues, conferring with your GM and your farm system people, and preparing for the rapidly approaching new season. Before you know it, you're giving your annual "Greetings" speech to your ballclub in Florida or Arizona.

All that I know, but the question about what might have been— or might still be—still gnaws at me, especially in late summer, with pennant and wild card races coming down to the wire and the postseason just around the corner. I see old friends and rivals doing battle with each other from the dugouts, and I can't help wondering what it would feel like to be in the thick of a stretch run again.

Funny, I don't necessarily feel that way in June. As Dusty, Scrap Iron, Ozzie, Charlie, and the boys are heading out to the yard, going through the same routine every day, I'm used to being in the Bahamas pulling in a wahoo or on some beautiful golf course scrambling for pars. Sure, like every serious fan, I watch games on TV and play out strategy in my mind, but I see inside the game and draw on my experience as a player. It's what I know. It's in my heart. But life has pulled me away from it—and it's become hard for me to return.

So, after watching the wild card Marlins do in the mighty Yankees in the 2003 World Series, I decided to make my move.

A few weeks earlier, during the celebration at Veterans Stadium before its demolition, I met with Phillies president David Montgomery and told him I was thinking about returning to the game—as a manager at some level or as a major league hitting coach. Through Tony La Russa, I had a relationship with the Cardinals, and I had

spoken informally with the Marlins, but I felt I had an obligation to
the Phillies. David had known of my interest in a major league position for a couple years. But he leaves the baseball operations decisions to general manager Ed Wade, and I wasn't high on Wade's
short list of names for job openings.

Now, while I may think I could walk in and take over a major
league team tomorrow, the men who make those decisions—men
like Ed Wade and most of his fellow GMs—don't necessarily share
that view. Can't blame 'em. Before 2004, I had nothing on my résumé that would lead anyone to conclude I had the right stuff to
manage a team. As a player, my dealings with the press had always
been dicey at best. I'd been a very high-profile player, known to be
a little self-centered, and not necessarily a strong people person
outside the clubhouse.

How could I work *for* someone?

How could I work "within" a team where my opinion counted
but wasn't the final one?

How in the hell could Mike Schmidt fit in as an everyday working stiff, dedicated to making an organization a winner without being the top dog?

Aside from these concerns, any GM hiring me—especially a
GM in Philadelphia—would have to factor in the political fallout
should I fall flat on my face and need to be canned. Firing a Hall
of Famer, especially one who has a statue at the stadium entrance,
could be tricky.

To view all this from a general manager's perspective is to realize
why so few high-profile players today ever get reasonable consideration for major league managerial jobs. In the last thirty years, only
two Hall of Fame players have managed in the majors: Yogi Berra
and Frank Robinson. Only one (Robbie) is a big league manager
today. Babe Ruth wanted to manage the Yankees when he retired;
they offered him the Newark Bears. See what I'm saying?

The general feeling in baseball seems to be that high-achieving ballplayers don't make good managers because they don't have the patience to work with players with lesser skills.

Realizing all this, I wanted to prove I was different. My itch was still there, and the Phillies gave me a chance to scratch it. I received a call in the fall of 2003 from Ed Wade saying that the Clearwater (Class A Florida State League) job was available: Would I be interested? He touched softly on some of the requirements and gave me a few days to think it over.

Understand that jobs like this one are pure gold to men with aspirations to careers as managers and coaches. A minor league job opens and a line forms, calls come from everywhere requesting interviews. This one was especially juicy: a good league with easy travel, a brand-new stadium, and a first-class organization.

Donna convinced me that I needed to work every day and to keep my mind active. Truer words were never spoken. But some questions remained: Did I have it in me? Could I discipline myself to dedicate the time and effort toward something like this, something as grueling and focused, something that required me to draw on my own experience to help a band of young men build their careers?

Man, this was a seven-month commitment, not a two-week spring training gig teaching hitting. I had to come back every day. No running off to play in a golf tournament somewhere. No heading out to the Bahamas for a week of fishing. And no managing from my couch in front of the TV. I had to sit on a hard bench and live, breathe, and teach baseball at a very basic level.

But I wasn't worried about the baseball part; that would be the easy part. I also had to become surrogate father to twenty-five young men. I had to set rules, work out lesson plans, dole out discipline, put out fires (and light a few others), listen to excuses, cure homesickness, manage expectations, deliver tough love, and help a motley crew of kids turn into a team of men.

Oh, yeah, and win a few games to boot.

I was hooked. I wasn't sure if I'd be good at deciding when to hit-and-run or pull a pitcher, but I was absolutely confident in my ability to communicate with and positively affect the lives of young men. I was also convinced that successfully completing this job would dramatically change other people's perception of me, in the event a major league managing opportunity came along.

So Donna and I put together a plan to exist on a far different schedule than we were used to for the next seven months. Then I went to Clearwater to interview with Ed Wade and the Phillies' minor league director, Mike Arbuckle, where I got a more detailed explanation of what the job entailed.

Mike outlined minor league organizational policies and schedules, emphasized some "horror" stories from past years, and generally painted a very clear picture that this was in no way, shape, or form a glamorous job. Oh, and the pay wasn't very good. There wasn't really anything about the job that should have been of interest to me, except the challenge it presented. The interview went well, and I was offered the position. I was to become the first Hall of Famer ever to manage in the minor leagues.

My first job was to strip myself of all the trappings that went with my perceived stature in the game. As I headed to spring training, I had to check my ego at the minor league clubhouse door. Of course, I would try to win games, but my real job was player development. I was one of forty or so instructors, scouts, and administrators responsible for developing talent so that the major league team could have a solid pool of young players from which to draw.

In spite of my usual bout with spring allergy attacks, the long days spent leaning on my fungo in the hot sun, and the drills that had to be done over and over and over, I truly enjoyed the experience of working with the kids. The ultimate kick for me was forming my team's roster. Of course, I had very little input as to which players ended up on my team; that was mostly up to Arbuckle and Bill Dancy, the director of the minor league camp. But every so often there'd be a utility kid or a bullpen pitcher you could fight for and maybe land. I lived for this.

Then the games started. Now I got to do a little managing—flash a sign, substitute a player, yell at an umpire, and generally get to know my team.

It felt right.

Working with my coaches was especially gratifying. Steve Schrenk (pitching coach), Manny Amador (hitting and third base coach), and Dan Roberts (first base coach) all became close friends. The bond that coaches develop in all sports is a wonderful thing. They helped me tremendously because they understood what I was trying to do, and where I needed a boost.

We worked our way through March and broke camp in early April, which, for the Clearwater Phillies, meant a hundred-yard walk to Bright House Networks Field, the Phillies' new spring training home. No disrespect to good old Jack Russell Stadium, where I spent nineteen springs, but this new ballpark added some serious charm to the job. Think 10,000-seat entertainment center with perfect field conditions and major league infrastructure, complete with a state-of-the-art workout center and a 20-foot-by-10-foot therapy pool where I could swim laps. We used only about half of the locker room, it was so big.

The team was a typical blend of white kids and Latinos, with only two African-American players. Atypically for a Class A team, a great many of my players were recycled minor league free agents—what are called "organizational" players, good kids who have been in the minors for several years and can help fill out a roster, but are no longer prospects. I had three or four pitchers and maybe two position players the Phillies brass considered legitimate prospects. They were to get my full attention in terms of playing time and extra work. If anyone had to be slighted, it would be the nonprospects. All those kids rocked at getting a paycheck for playing a game they loved. Most understood at some level that their chances of making it to the big leagues fell somewhere between slim and none, but none ever gave up hope.

You saw *Bull Durham*, right? That's the way it was—and probably always will be. Minus Susan Sarandon.

One day in spring camp, I was asked to sit in on a few releases, so I'd be familiar with the process. I sat quietly as the camp director told two players it was over for them. One was cordial, thanked everyone for the opportunity, shook hands, and left. The other, a big pitcher, stood there with a look on his face like he was ready to kill. The silence grew deafening, but finally he calmed down and asked if some calls could be made on his behalf. It was scary. He could have filled the room with uppercuts in a second, and I would have been a candidate to get one, even though I was just an observer.

My turn came early in the season, as I was ordered to release our backup catcher, Edgar Cruz. Nice young kid, quiet and hardworking, with the organization for a few years—but expendable. The tough thing was that Edgar's wife was expecting to deliver their first child in a day or so, and this would leave him with a new baby and no job. Being new at this sort of thing made it hard; I took it personally and was concerned for Edgar. All I could think of doing was to emphasize that now he could go home and spend time with his new baby and wife. I bought him a present for the baby and told him it would all work out for the best. We hugged, cried, and said goodbye.

So many human stories: kids in trouble late at night, kids failing drug tests, kids getting injured, kids insisting on testing dress code rules; having to fine kids who barely had enough money to live on, having to release our chapel leader, a journeyman pitcher whom I got to know and love.

And then there was Easy Ramirez.

On May 23 in Vero Beach, I received notice from Philadelphia to send Elizardo "Easy" Ramirez, a polished young twenty-year-old right-hander, to the big club right away; they might need him to start against the Padres in two days. You can imagine the thrill this was going to be for him, but what about me? It's not often that a manager gets to tell one of his players that he's going up to the "show."

Anyway, Ramirez speaks only a few words of English, so when I bring him into my office I ask his friend, Alfredo Simon, to come along to interpret. "Congratulations, you're going up to Philadelphia," I begin. "Vincent Padilla has a sore elbow, and they want you to be ready to pitch day after tomorrow against the Padres." Easy looks at me, then at his friend, who repeats what I said in Spanish. By nature a relaxed, poised kid, Easy looks at me calmly and says, "No way. You bullshit me." I say to Alfredo, "Tell him this is no bullshit. He needs to pack up, *right now,* and get ready to catch a flight to Philly."

The look on Easy's face is something to behold. I'll never forget that moment. It was a look that made my entire year. He was almost in shock. I open the door, call the team together, and announce that Easy is headed to Philly and that he might start against the Padres the day after tomorrow. The team lets out a spontaneous roar that could be heard all the way across Florida in Clearwater.

(Rough translation: "One of us got the call! Maybe I'll be next!")

Easy had no way of calling home to the Dominican Republic, so I lent him my cell phone and told him to call whomever he wanted and talk as long as he wanted to. He said, "I'm going to tell everyone, even my donkey!" Easy went to Philadelphia, where he watched as Padilla warmed up, felt no discomfort, and pitched that day after all. So Easy never got that start, but he did pitch in seven games for the Phillies in 2004. Subsequently he was sent to Cincinnati in a trade, never to see the lower minors again.

Much as I enjoyed working with the kids, we weren't a good team. We prepared well and we played hard every day, but we just didn't have the horses. We were outmanned just about every game. Opposing teams would come to our park and make it look small, which it was. It was a long, long year in terms of wins (51) and losses (85). Say what you want about player development, kids need to win their fair share of games, and we didn't have enough talent to do that.

For me, it became very hard to take. I was unable to manage to win, because player development took priority. If a certain hitter or bullpen pitcher was hot, I wasn't able to take full advantage of it, because the hot guy meant a prospect might not get his scheduled innings.

One game in Daytona, we had a lead and Ryan Hutchinson is walking through them in middle relief. No way am I taking him out; he's got six straight outs and hasn't broken a sweat. But earlier in the day I'd been informed that Francisco Butto hadn't pitched in three days and needed to get in the game for two innings. So out comes Hutchinson, in comes Butto for the eighth and ninth. He gets wild, loads the bases, and gives up the longest grand slam I've ever seen. Personally, I felt winning the game would have meant more to the team's development than pitching a couple of innings did to Butto's, but that wasn't my call, and that sort of thing happened numerous times throughout the summer.

The hard thing—and I'd been warned about this before I took the job—was that what I brought to the job in terms of teaching kids how to play to win was being wasted. We might do great things to get a lead, but not being able to put the right people in to seal the win often prevented us from reaping the rewards of our efforts.

I thought I did a decent job, considering the circumstances. I tended to over-manage, meaning I controlled late inning at-bats, putting on the hit-and-run and sending my runners a lot. We had to do things to create offense because we had very little power and only two major league prospects in the lineup. I did my job as directed—okay, I could probably have been a bit more tuned in to the "development" thing at times. But with the hand my staff and I were dealt, we did a lot of good things. Most importantly, several key players got better on our watch, and that's the bottom line.

Remember your best teachers when you were a kid? The ones who grabbed and kept your attention, sparked your imagination, and got you to focus on your job, which was to live up to your potential? I think you'd agree that they were the unsung (and usually underpaid) heroes who played a huge role in making you what you are today.

Well, baseball has their equivalent: managers and coaches in the minor leagues, especially Class A and AA ball.

I always knew, without thinking much about it, that managers at the minor league level (and coaches at *all* levels) were treated like second-class citizens on the pay scale. But after spending seven months in their world as a manager in A-ball in 2004, I have developed a strong conviction that that's a dumb way to run a business.

Look, the Phillies—like all other major league teams—invest several million dollars in a top young draftee, and they expect him to develop into a major league talent in four years. At any given time, a lower minor league team in a major league team's system might have four or five players of that caliber on its roster. They are nothing less than the future heart and soul of the big league club. So explain to me how a parent club can invest over $10 million in these players, and then hire a manager to teach them the fundamentals of the game and, more important, how to behave and think like a major leaguer—and pay that manager a grand salary of $30,000?

I am not saying the guys currently holding these positions, at about that salary, are doing a poor job. Quite the contrary; the guys I know bust their butts teaching the game *and* trying to win. But imagine the experience, the talent, and the wisdom an organization could buy for eight to ten times that amount.

How many qualified men, with serious major league experience, would be candidates for long-term positions in player development if the salary fit the position? Offer $250,000 to manage a Class A team and see how many former major league All-Stars call for an interview. Count me in!

My point: in an industry in which the word "million" is thrown around like chump change, why don't the people who run it upgrade the compensation levels of the key individuals directly responsible for nurturing their most important asset?

The season ended with a storm—make that *two* storms, Charley and Frances. On August 14 Hurricane Charley made landfall in Boca Grande, 150 miles south of our stadium. It shut the league down for several days, and caused Sarasota and Fort Meyers to alter their schedules. Our stadium became a hurricane shelter. Once we resumed play, we got about two weeks in before Frances came along. Season over.

It was also over for Larry Bowa, who was fired as Phillies manager in late September with two games left. Larry got the typical raw deal that a manager of an underachieving team often gets. His record when he got the ax was 85 and 75—10 games over .500! And he got them there without his closer and cleanup hitter most of the year. But Larry was said to be too volatile and too emotional, which put too much pressure on his players.

Whatever; it's always easier to fire one manager than the twenty-five guys who are making millions. But fingering Bowa as the reason for the Phillies' disappointing 2004 season is letting the players off the hook. It's saying that they're not at fault, that they needed an outside motivational source to perform as winners, and that Bowa didn't motivate them.

Bullshit. A major league player shouldn't need an external motivational source. Motivation should come from within. Or it should come every fifteen days, when he cashes his paycheck. With few exceptions, managers aren't the reasons teams fail. Larry Bowa wasn't one of those exceptions.

The upside—for me, at least—was that I'd at least be a candidate to take over as Phillies manager. Things were falling into place. Or so I thought.

Football, basketball, and baseball teams are headed up by coaches. Baseball has a manager. What's the difference?

Simple. In the other three team sports, the head coach brings with him a "system" for playing the game. The playbook, the X's and O's, the game plan he's developed and used in every job on his way to the top. A system evolved from past playing and coaching experience.

In baseball, of course, there's no playbook. All teams have the same plays ready for the same situations. Sac bunt, hit-and-run, steal, squeeze—they're in every team's arsenal, and they're employed in the same situations. They all have similar information data banks with tendencies (hitters and pitchers). They all have similar scouting reports. It's the same game everywhere, left up to the players to play. It's a team game built around a series of one-on-one confrontations between hitter and pitcher.

Other things being equal, the teams with the best talent and the fewest injuries should win. So what does a manager do? What does he bring to the table?

He manages people. Baseball is a journey where twenty-five men travel around the country for six months and play a game almost every day, the same routine over and over. It's a grind, and the person in charge of order and control is the manager. His job is to keep the show running smoothly and the individual parts working together, no matter what negative elements surface.

The manager is judged on wins and losses—period. It doesn't matter whether he's liked or disliked, quiet or loud, emotional or unemotional, experienced or inexperienced. Whatever he is, he's "right" if he wins, and "wrong" if he loses. He oversees twenty-five guys getting paid a combined $70, 80, 90 million or more. If they don't win five of every eight games, it's his fault, and he gets the ax.

But another team will likely hire him because . . . well, because that's the way baseball has always done it. Why? Probably because GMs feel safer betting on experience than on potential. Failure with one team is rarely a deterrent to being hired by another. If you manage in the big leagues, you are officially a big league manager. You have the key qualification that fits into a GM's comfort zone: experience.

Good experience? Bad experience? Doesn't matter as much as you might think. There's always a pool of recycled managers looking for job openings every off-season, and the ones who get passed over bide time as bench coaches or color analysts on ESPN or local cable, and wait till next year.

GMs fire managers because they have to do something to change the environment, not because deep down they always believe the manager is at fault. Then they hire a former manager, who was fired by some other team, and the circle goes round and round. Trust me, it's seldom, if ever, the manager's fault if a team fails. He's just the easiest to blame.

Sparky Anderson, Earl Weaver, Tommy Lasorda, Chuck Tanner, Dick Williams, Whitey Herzog, Tony La Russa, and Bobby Cox were the great managers of my era. What was it about those guys? Was it a special X-quality they shared? Was it just a question of showing up with great talent? What special traits would a great manager possess?

Here's what eighteen seasons as a player under six managers, five years as a hitting coach in spring training, and a year managing in Class A has taught me about what it takes to be a big league manager.

• • •

A manager must command the respect from his players. Everybody knows that. No respect, no leadership.

But let's go beyond the knee-jerk reaction: "I respect him because he's the manager." Think beyond mere respect for the office. Think about a level of respect that derives from an external reason: a World Series ring or two (or more), a significant tenure as a high-level coach, or a long, distinguished playing career. Personally, I'd be most likely to respect someone who's faced the music before, who can relate to the failures that come with the game, and who knows from experience the pressures his players are under.

Respect is a two-way street. A great manager must make abundantly clear that he respects his players. If his players sense that, they'll run through walls for him, be challenged to achieve by the mere fact of his presence, and believe in his decisions and demands on them.

Another key trait of a great manager is the ability to control his emotions. A manager has numerous opportunities to blow his stack in your typical ball game. Being able to remain calm and positive in the teeth of adversity is an absolute necessity. Everyone in the dugout checks out the manager's reaction when things go sour. Any display of excessive anger, disgust, or disappointment adds to the burden of the player's failure. Whatever he's feeling inside, a manager must convey to his players the sense that all is well, that somebody will get the key hit or make the right pitch next time.

A manager must have a feel for the flow of a ball game. Every game has momentum shifts, and a manager has to feel them and tilt them his team's way whenever possible. A manager who understands momentum will school his team on the value of doing the little things consistently. If you move runners up, put the ball in play, throw to the right base, and run the bases correctly, you're more likely to keep on momentum's good side. If you feel momentum sitting in your dugout, you need to keep it there. If "Mo" is sitting in the other guys' dugout, you need to get it back. A good manager always knows where it is. A great one knows how to get it back.

Momentum's a factor customarily associated with other sports, particularly football and basketball, but I've always been tuned into it in baseball. I feel the rhythm of the game. A pitcher working too slow, a basic play botched in a key situation, an outstanding defensive play, an umpire's call—things like that can shift a baseball game's momentum. And get this: A home run can sometimes kill your offensive momentum.

Say your team's down by four runs in the ninth with one on and one out, and your guy hits a two-run homer. *Great!* Think again. A homer in that situation can kill the momentum of the inning. Now you're down by two, only the bases are empty. You'd be better off with a walk than a home run in that situation, because the walk keeps the rally alive and lets the momentum build. As manager, I'd flash the take sign in 1–0, 2–0, and 3–1 counts in a situation like that, hoping for the walk, not the home run.

Old Mo's a fickle force: A manager's got to know how to keep it working for him.

Experience? A little way down on my list, you'll notice, because I have very little. Sure, experience in doing the things managers do is valuable—things like making out lineups, sending runners, putting on the hit-and-run, arguing with umpires, knowing the rules, and leading a staff. Today, much of the detail work is done by the bench coach, who's really a de facto assistant manager. In the end, the manager makes the call, but most game decisions—notably pitching moves—are reviewed with coaches. Many are blocked out before the game according to the system the manager and his staff have created.

Experience improves a manager's sense of timing. I remember not having given enough warning to a pinch hitter, not having a pinch runner ready in time, and waiting too long to get a pitcher up—all things that experience helps you avoid. Not even the most experienced manager is immune to these kinds of miscues, of course, but they're less likely to happen today because of the input of the bench coach.

A manager must be able to handle the media. By that I mean deal with the media in a way that benefits—and sometimes protects—his players. The media have a larger, more forceful presence in some towns than others, and a manager's ability to handle their demands is essential in preventing negative issues from affecting his team's performance. Emphasizing hidden moments in a game, explaining important plays that seemed routine, highlighting tough at-bats and extraordinary individual effort, and never, never, ever criticizing players are key things a manager has to keep in mind when dealing with the media.

Oh, and one more thing: Tell the truth. Lie to the press and they'll kill you. Be straight with them and they'll respect you.

The sixth and most important attribute of a good manager—and this one's a straight fastball right down the middle—is the ability to communicate. To be a good manager, you must be a good communicator. That means being able to talk *to* your players, not *at* them. You need to work at relating to them, but at the same time, you need to keep a respectful distance. Keep them loose. Keep them in a positive frame of mind. Show you care about them personally. You can't just stroll out of your office into the clubhouse one day a week and fake it; you have to have a consistent presence.

But you also have to be sensitive to the times when players need to be left alone. The clubhouse belongs to them; players respect a manager who makes it clear he understands that.

A manager's message to his players must be simple, direct, and unambiguous: "Prepare—concentrate—execute." (Plus, of course, the ever-popular "Be on time.") Few managers would find fault with that message. But I would make one crucial addition: "Spread the love." That's right: Spread as much love as possible throughout the team.

Love? *Love?* I can hear you right now—"What the hell does love have to do with winning baseball games?"

Just this: Love is the most powerful motivator of all. Remember what I said about the outpouring of love from my teammates when I announced my retirement? Knowing that Dutch and Von and the other guys loved me was the most powerful feeling I'd ever had in baseball. Joe Ehrmann, former Colts All-Pro defensive lineman, says in *Season of Life,* his book about a successful high school football team, that a team built on love will ultimately perform at the highest level possible. Larry Brown, during a time-out in the final seconds of the final game of the 2005 NBA Championship, told his Pistons team only that he loved them.

Why do teams suddenly find "chemistry" or get in the "zone"? Because they don't fear failure, because they're letting it flow, because they know the bounces will eventually go their way. No matter what the outcome, they'll feel good about themselves, because there's love in the air. Love liberates a free-spirited approach to playing the game. In that kind of team environment, a player asked to bunt at an unusual time will go, "Cool, watch this blueprint bunt." Absent that, he's more like, "How can that idiot make me bunt now?"

How a player reacts depends on the existence of a *team* environment that encourages him to set aside his personal agenda. And that environment depends on the manager's ability to communicate—and instill—a foundation of love.

Communicating this philosophy is hard. After all, baseball rewards individual performance. But if a master communicator can create an environment full of love and mutual respect, and if it's fun to come to work every day, then even on a team with only "decent" talent, players will play to their highest potential.

• • •

I'd be tough to hire as a manager. I understand that. Your typical manager candidate goes after a job hard—whatever the job, wherever it is—because he has the passion, the desire, and the need. For me, it's passion, yes; desire maybe; and need, not so much.

Once upon a time, Hall of Fame players turned routinely to managing after they hung up their spikes: Walter Johnson, Rogers Hornsby, Tris Speaker, Joe Cronin, Frankie Frisch, Lou Boudreau, Red Schoendienst, Ted Williams, Yogi Berra, and Frank Robinson. Part of it had to do with a passion for baseball—those guys were baseball men for life. And part of it had to do with money: Baseball was the way they made a living.

Do you think for one minute that Alex Rodriguez, who has as much passion for the game as anybody, is going to be out looking for a managing job after he retires? I'm guessing that, like me, he knows he could do it, and he'd like other people to know it, but he certainly won't need the job. That guy'll never need *any* job the rest of his life, at least not financially.

Starting around the mid-1980s, a lot of baseball players started retiring as wealthy men. They left the game looking for freedom and comfort, not for a baseball job. They could afford to walk away from the constant travel, the separation from family, the day-to-day grind, the pressure, the loss of privacy, the demands of autograph seekers, the aches and pains. They could afford to walk away from baseball. And most did.

Problem is, you can't spend a couple of decades of your life totally immersed in something so intense as major league baseball, reach its pinnacle as a player, and not have it in your blood for the rest of your life. You can hang up your spikes, but you can't hang up your essence.

What happens if you want to come back? What happens if your passion beats common sense in extra innings? New suits run the front offices, rosters are filled with guys you've seen play only on TV, and your only link to the game becomes your highlight reel. You face a big hurdle. You know you have exactly what it takes to do the job, but no way of proving it—unless you find someone strong enough to see beyond a résumé and make a leap of faith that talent, ideas, and energy are at least as important as experience.

A baseball player of a certain caliber—a Gary Carter, an Eddie Murray, a Johnny Bench, a Mike Schmidt—can return to the game after being away still equipped with the respect and the knowledge he earned as a player. And a player like that has certainly proved, over the course of a Hall of Fame career, that he knows how to lead.

Sure, I was disappointed in not being considered for the Phillies job in 2004, even though I understood at the time why I wasn't. Their number one priority was prior experience managing in the big leagues, and I had none. End of story. End of story.

Or is it?

Times change. Situations change. But one thing hasn't changed: I haven't forgotten how to win.

It's in the blood.

14 Still the Best Game in Town

Baseball is booming. Attendance went up in 2005 for the tenth straight season. Television income is *way* up: last season, MLB received $141 million from ESPN for rights to regular season games; for the next five seasons, that figure jumps to an average of $296 million per year. (*Not* counting the postseason.) Licensing income has skyrocketed, with future partners queuing up to sign on the dotted line. Franchise values continue to climb, with the pending purchase of the Washington Nationals extending a decades-long streak of price increases for the privilege of owning a major league ballclub. And on a qualitative note, baseball fans are getting to enjoy what is without doubt the greatest, deepest collection of pure talent ever to play in any era.

So what's the problem?

You know *one* answer: steroids.

The number one issue facing the game today is whether the MLBPA and the Commissioner's Office can make the new, stricter testing and penalty program for performance-enhancing drugs work to rid the game of steroids.

As a former player, I respect the role the MLBPA has historically played in protecting players' rights. The successful battles the union waged for free agency and against collusion, for example, benefited the players *and* the game. But over the last fifteen years, the use of performance-enhancing drugs became widespread because Major League Baseball's drug program had no teeth. I am personally gratified that Donald Fehr and my union have now stepped up to take a principled, positive stand in support of the new, stronger program aimed squarely at kicking steroids out of baseball.

Ample evidence suggests that the spotlight on steroid use the last couple of years is having an effect, even without stricter testing. In 2005, nine players hit 40 or more home runs. In 2000, sixteen did. Last season, twenty-seven players drove in 100 or more runs. Five years ago, the figure was fifty-three. And many players are physically smaller than they were a couple of years ago.

That good news is encouraging, but this is no time to relax. Somewhere out there, someone's in a lab trying to cook up some juice that can't be detected by today's testing methods. And if we know anything, we know not to bet against technology. Baseball's taken a major first step, but this is no time for complacency.

I applaud baseball's new drug policy for the simple reason that 50–100–Life says loud and clear that you mean business. Test positive once and you lose almost a *third* of your salary—and a big chunk of market value if you should ever declare for free agency. (What team would take the risk?) That's a language everybody understands. Going forward, players looking for an edge—that is, every player in the game—will be scared to look for it in anabolic steroids. The absence of strict penalties for steroid use practically invited a player looking for an edge to cross the line. Now, with strict penalties in place, a player would have to be barking mad to go anywhere near the No Steroids line.

It's much like your kids knowing that if they wander out of the neighborhood, and get caught, they'll be punished seriously. Trust me, if it's no ice cream before bed, they'll risk it. If it's a week in their room with no TV, they'll hang around home.

Keep in mind that most players in the Steroid Era did not use performance-enhancing drugs. That's worth repeating: *Most players in the Steroid Era did not use performance-enhancing drugs.*

Non-users knew or at least suspected which of their teammates did use, but they honored the clubhouse code and kept quiet. Though they never went public, a growing number began to make clear through their player reps that they wanted a level playing field and that they would accept stricter testing and sterner penalties. They were in the majority—a very, very quiet majority.

Now, finally, that majority, through the MLBPA, has spoken up. And I like what I hear.

Steroid use is the number one problem facing major league baseball today, but there are others, and there will be more. Given the record of the last thirty years—relentless conflict between the players and the owners—isn't it time for a fresh look at how baseball is governed?

The Commissioner of Baseball is employed by the owners. However much he—Bud Selig—might pontificate about representing "the Game," he is answerable to the people who hired him and can fire him: the owners.

The Executive Director of the Major League Baseball Players Association is employed by the players. He—Donald Fehr—doesn't even pretend to represent anybody or anything besides the people who hire him and can fire him: the players.

Together, these two entities determine baseball's policies through an inherently adversarial procedure: collective bargaining. It works, when it does, when the two sides manage to hammer out a compromise on an issue they disagree on. When it doesn't work, you have a strike (1981, 1994) or a stalemate (a drug policy with-out teeth, at least until 2005).

What if a third entity, one highly respected by fans, players, and owners alike, had a role—a strong role—in helping give direction to the two sides?

The Otsego Committee could fill that role. Never heard of the Ot-sego Committee? Not surprising, because it doesn't exist. But it should.

The Hall of Fame's current sixty-one-man "active" roster—that is, those of us who aren't dead—spans nearly seventy years of experi-ence in the game. No other body is more entitled to speak for the good of the game. What better resource could there be for baseball to tap for informed, disinterested recommendations on a myriad of issues from rule changes to drug testing to international expansion?

The Otsego Committee, a seven-member committee of Hall of Famers, nominated and selected by their peers, would act as a study group and adviser to Major League Baseball. Terms of service would be limited to two years. Two new members would be added each year at the prestigious Sunday night dinner of Induction Weekend. The com-mittee would have a support staff and a budget funded in equal mea-sure by the MLBPA and the Office of the Commissioner of Baseball.

The Otsego Committee's reports and recommendations, based on independent research and polling of the Hall of Fame membership at large, would be presented directly to the MLBPA and the commis-sioner. A study could be initiated upon request from the MLBPA or the Commissioner's Office, or commenced on its own by the OC. Had it been in place since 2000, the Otsego Committee would have studied and offered position papers on the following: labor issues, drug testing policies, the Pete Rose case, HOF voting policy, Steroid Era players and the HOF, and numerous other issues.

Take the Pete Rose case. The commissioner could have de-ferred to the Otsego Committee, which would then have inter-viewed Bud, Pete, and any other pertinent individuals, deliberated, and proposed a recommended course of action. Case closed. No one would argue with a committee of Hall of Fame members on this issue—nor, most likely, on any baseball issue.

Players, fans, and owners alike hold Hall of Famers in the highest regard. Why not give them a strong voice in directing the game?

Abolish the designated hitter? Nonsense. I say extend it to the National League.

I know, I know. You're going, What's number 20 thinking? Has he lost his freakin' mind? Is this the same hard-shell baseball purist who's been grumbling about the sanctity of America's Game since page 1?

Look, if you'd asked me before I started writing this book how I felt about the DH, I'd have said—unequivocally—let's get rid of it!

I was wrong. In thinking about the larger context of how baseball's future is shaping up, I'm now saying—just as unequivocally—let's level the playing field!

That's right, when you cancel out all the pluses and minuses of the DH—and you know them every bit as well as I do, unless you've spent the last twenty baseball seasons on Mars—it comes down to making sure the two leagues are playing the same game.

Couldn't that be done by *abolishing* the DH in the American League? Sure, but that ain't going to happen, not so long as David Ortiz has a bat in his hands. Or so long as Donald Fehr has union jobs to protect. Or American League owners have bleachers to fill.

But there's another, more positive reason for extending the DH to the NL, and it's this: Fans dig the long ball. And runs, *lots* of runs. If there's one thing we've learned from the last couple of decades, it's that fans love high-scoring slugfests. And unless something's changed since I left the game, it's still the fans who pay the bills.

And you know what else? It's time to start looking at the pitcher as exactly what he is, a defensive player. His job is to stop runs from scoring, period. He has enough to do without ever having to pick up a bat. He's already the focal point of the game. A pitcher with a bat in his hands is like a pig with a violin—he doesn't know what to do with the damn thing.

Last fall, Roger Clemens and John Smoltz squared off in game two of the NL Division Series between Houston and Atlanta. Who wasn't looking forward to seeing two great competitors pitch against each other in an October game? Unfortunately, we also faced the prospect of having to watch them both hit. Now, Smoltz is a decent hitter (for a pitcher), but Clemens is no hitter at all, having spent most of his career in the American League. Going into that kind of matchup, wouldn't you have preferred to see forty-three-year-old Clemens trying to throw his splitter past forty-seven-year-old DH Julio Franco, and Smoltz challenging DH Jeff Bagwell with high heat? As it worked out, Clemens got roughed up and the game wasn't close (7–1, Braves), but had it been, those two guys could have gone all the way. Take your pick: seven or eight near-certain outs or a dangerous hitter facing a great pitcher in a postseason game?

Yes, I know—Dontrelle Willis can handle a bat. So could Bob Gibson and Steve Carlton. But putting any of those guys in the lineup instead of a real hitter would be like giving me the ball and saying "Go get 'em, Mike. You're starting today." Admit it, a pitcher's at-bat means one thing: bathroom break. Remove him from the lineup, and every inning is a potential rally.

So let's take a bold step into the future.

Let's *really* level the playing field.

Let a designated hitter bat—in both leagues.

So what about the short power alleys, high-tech bats, jazzed-up balls, and shrinking strike zones you were bitching about earlier, number 20? What should be done about them?

Nothing.

You're not going to tear down the comfortable, aesthetically pleasing new ballparks just because they're hitter-friendly. I hope we never witness the demise of Wrigley or Fenway, but without exception the new ballparks are better than the things they replaced. Anybody really miss the Astrodome? Not me.

The new bats are lighter and harder than the bats of a couple of decades ago. They'll probably continue to get lighter and harder. Anything wrong with that? Not in my book.

Balls will always be under suspicion when home run totals jump, because manufacturing standards are higher and you get fewer duds coming off the line. Today's balls are tighter than they used to be. But by a magnitude sufficient to distort the game? Even if you think so—and I don't—you'd have to figure out a way to prove it, scientifically, and nobody's ever been able to do that. And wouldn't it take some of the fun out of the game if pitchers stopped complaining about the ball?

The strike zone? Well, I don't think anybody will argue that it's not a lot smaller than what the rules say it is, so I'm making an exception to my "Nothing" answer to the question "What should be done?" I think the real zone should be pushed closer to the rule book zone. Maybe in stages, over a few years, so as not to disrupt the game unduly. Maybe start in the low minors and add a year until you get to the majors. This would do more than any other single change to restore the historic pitcher-hitter balance, because it would give pitchers a new weapon that has disappeared from the game: the high strike. It would also mean Nolan Ryan would come out of retirement.

So we have these four factors in today's game—shorter power alleys in most of the newer ballparks (for sure), bats that are lighter and harder (for sure), a hotter ball (maybe), a smaller strike zone (absolutely)—that have changed over the last thirty years. Taken together, they've affected the way baseball is played, with more home runs and higher scores than ever before in its history. The result is that the integrity of historical performance records is now in jeopardy. And, except for bringing the strike zone back a little closer to what it once was, number 20 is saying we should do *nothing*?

Not exactly. I am saying we should steer clear of asterisks, footnotes, qualifying statements, and related nonsense in the record books. Somebody swats 75? So be it. Barry Bonds sails past Hank Aaron and cracks the 800-homer barrier? Good for you, Barry. Slap an asterisk on either number? No way.

But I'm also saying this: *keep in mind the changes*. All I ask is that fans, Hall of Fame voters, journalists, everybody who follows baseball just *keep in mind the changes* in the game over the last thirty years when weighing the accomplishments of today's (and tomorrow's) players against those from players of an earlier era. Be a smarter, more educated fan. Salute the new records as they're set. But *keep in mind* the changes in the game that helped make them possible.

Consider this: Hank Aaron averaged 33 home runs a year over twenty-three full seasons. Mark McGwire averaged 39 over fifteen. (I'm throwing out the eighteen games McGwire played in 1986.) That's an 18 percent differential. Would Mark have hit 18 percent more home runs than Hank had they both played in the same era? No disrespect to Mark, but I don't think so. Stick in a footnote whenever you run their stats side by side? Of course not. Just *keep in mind* not only *what* Hank did but *when*.

The change in baseball over the last thirty years that concerns me most is the decline in loyalty.

Not fan-team loyalty. Fans are still fiercely loyal to their teams. The only way you could tell a Cubs fan in 2005 from one in, say, 1935 is by what was on his head: The first guy would be sporting a Cubs cap, the second a gray fedora. Otherwise, they'd have the same hangdog, disappointed, wait-till-next-year, we'll-figure-out-a-new-way-to-lose face that Cubs fans have put on every season since time began. And you think Red Sox fans are any less devoted now than when Teddy Ballgame and Yaz and Pudge were coming up short? Pay a visit to Red Sox Nation and learn otherwise.

And not fan-player loyalty, either. It seems like it would be hard, especially for kids, to stay loyal to players who, because of free agency, tend to come and go like platoons on a football field. It's obviously not, or the sale of logo gear would be down, not up. (Which one of six Gary Sheffield jerseys would fetch more on eBay?) Fans, *especially* kids, have adapted quite nicely, thank you very much. Your guys are your guys, until they're not your guys anymore. And then you find some new guys. Hard for an old-timer like me to get his head around, but easy for today's fan.

No, the loyalty I'm talking about is the loyalty within a clubhouse, the loyalty that used to—in the days before free agency—bond a team together. Before 1976, that sort of loyalty was a given. Most players came up in the same organization and played on the same team together their entire careers. The loyalty they felt toward one another was a natural, organic thing. Players dreaded being traded. They had roots in their communities. They saw their best friends at work every day. Their families knew one another.

Free agency changed all that. Suddenly a guy could choose between lifetime financial security and loyalty to twenty-four other guys, all of whom would soon be facing the same choice. You know what happened.

Look, I'd be the last person to knock free agency. Because of it, I got the best of both worlds: financial security *and* the chance to stay with my guys, my team. And I don't mean to say players don't become friends and bond together with the common goal of winning. It's just that their bond is not as deeply rooted. Your double-play partner this year could be trying to knock you into left field next year.

Whose hat will Roger Clemens wear on Induction Day in Cooperstown?

Fact is, today's players never experienced the sense of clubhouse loyalty, so there's nothing for them to miss. And if they did, one look at their bimonthly pay stub would ease the pain.

But I have to say that there is one other type of loyalty that concerns me: the loyalty that fans have to the *game*.

By that I mean, how today's fans understand and respect a game that is a century old. Do you respect its history? Its legends? Its inner fabric?

I know you do, certainly compared with fans of NFL football and NBA basketball, because those fans can appreciate their games to the fullest without knowing their history. Baseball fans *need* their history. And I fear that for some—for many—that history is in danger of slipping away.

You see, erosion is an insidious process. Without quite knowing what happened, you look up one day and something is gone forever.

Baseball's soul can't be measured by stats—Attendance up! Scoring up! Everything's okay! (Too simplistic. Maybe misleading.) Maybe it can't be measured at all. But despite a lot of good signs, I am nonetheless concerned that baseball's soul is in peril.

What happens when the excitement of the new ballparks wears off? What happens when fans, pulled in different directions by everything from hand-held video games to who-knows-what technology of the future, start demanding more features at the ol' ballpark? What happens when, in the post–Steroid Era, home runs and high scoring tail off? What happens when the game on the field no longer suffices?

It's not enough for us fans to be loyal to our team. It's not enough for us to be loyal to our favorite players. We also must remain loyal to baseball's *soul*.

I believe we have a responsibility to convey to the next generation of fans the inner beauty of the game. We must help them see that a perfectly executed sacrifice bunt followed by a sacrifice fly is just as powerful, just as valuable, just as worthy of their respect as a

400-foot home run. We must be sure they understand that a player who hits .260 with no power but plays great defense and hustles on every play is a valuable asset to his team. We must show them how much more there is to love than long home runs. We must help them discover the little things that so easily get overlooked in all the hype and hoopla and swagger, the little things that add up to a whole that's so much greater than the sum of its parts.

The *game*.

America's game.

Baseball has changed over the last thirty years. No surprise, because so has the world. But changes in baseball can be tough to deal with emotionally because when we think of the game, we think of it the way it was when we first discovered it. And those times are frozen in our memories, immutable to change. They are, but the game is not.

Baseball is no longer defined by a bunch of scruffy kids coming together on their own every summer afternoon for a pickup game in which any ball hit to right field was an out because there wasn't a right fielder. Baseball today is defined by Little League, which has become quite a big business.

Baseball used to be played in bandboxes (with grown-up power alleys!) like old Crosley Field in Cincinnati, where my dreams started when I was a little boy. It was played by men who resembled firemen, tough men, honorable men, men who would rub your head and say, "Hey, kid, doing well in school?" along the rail at third base. There was something simple about the game then, something that seems to have left it—for good.

And maybe that's okay. Back in the day, baseball was—almost literally—the only game in town. Now it's not, not by a long shot. And maybe we don't need it to be.

People's lives today are much more complicated, with many more choices, than ours were back in that frozen-forever time when we first discovered baseball. That's true if you're fifty-five or seventy-five or twenty-five. The only difference is in the details. But people adapt to change, so they adapt to changes in baseball. Today's fans seem perfectly content with "their" baseball. It's only us old folks who feel a twinge of longing for a different kind of baseball.

I say we need to get over it.

Anybody know who's going for the Phillies tomorrow?

ACKNOWLEDGMENTS

Many, many people contribute to the making of a life, a lot of them without even knowing it. The same goes for a book, especially one that draws so heavily on the experiences of a single lifetime, as this one does. So here is a partial list of people who deserve a ton of credit for what appears in these pages. Thanks, one and all:

- Scott Waxman and Farley Chase of the Waxman Agency encouraged and guided me every step of the way. Many thanks.
- Editor David Hirshey at HarperCollins and his wingman Miles Doyle asked a lot of tough questions and pushed me hard to find the answers. They are true masters of the art of saying, "Good job" and "You gotta turn this thing inside out" in the same breath.
- To my friend and coauthor Glen Waggoner, I'd like to extend a special thank you. Glen, you made this project fun. You educated me on the fine art of writing as we pulled the manuscript together. Your insights about baseball made a tremendous difference in the final copy. You, my man, were a great partner.

Maybe someday we can do it again. The "dirty" martinis are on me in 2006.

- Tenacious researcher Jon Wank kept a bunch of ground balls from getting through the infield. And the ones that did get by? Score them E-5.
- My friend and agent Warren Greene is a consummate professional and fierce defender of my best interests, even when I haven't fully grasped what they are. Thanks for everything, Warren.
- Arthur Rosenberg, a lifelong friend and protector of my family's financial affairs. Thanks for always being there.
- A tip of my Phillies cap to the Philadelphia Phillies organization, from Bill Giles and David Montgomery to former GM Ed Wade to Public Relations Director Larry Shenk (along with Debbie Nocito and Susan Ingersoll), for their constant efforts on my behalf.
- To trainers Jeff Cooper and Mark Anderson, whose dedication was matched only by their talents. I'd never have made it through 2,404 games without you.
- To coaches Bobby Wine, Mike Ryan, and Billy DeMars for making me into a hitter.
- To managers Danny Ozark, Paul Owens, Dallas Green, Pat Corrales, John Felske, and Nick Leyva, who put up with a lot and taught me even more.
- To my mentors: Dave Cash, Garry Maddox, Dick Allen, Pete Rose.
- To my Hall of Fame teammates: Steve Carlton, Joe Morgan, Tony Perez—and, someday, Pete.
- To a special friend, Tug McGraw.
- To a great bunch of guys who made the Phillies clubhouse my home away from home: Steve Bedrosian, Bob Boone, Larry Bowa, Larry Christenson, Darren Daulton, John Denny, Bob

Dernier, Bo Diaz, Ed Farmer, Greg Gross, Kevin Gross, Von Hayes, Al Holland, Davey Johnson, Jim Kaat, Jerry Koosman, Jim Lonborg, Greg Luzinski, Gary Matthews, Bake McBride, Tim McCarver, Willie Montanez, Keith Moreland, Lance Parrish, Shane Rawley, Ron Reed, Dick Ruthven, Juan Samuel, Lonnie Smith, Dave Stewart, Tony Taylor, Kent Tekulve, Milt Thompson, John Vukovich, and Glenn Wilson.

Now, in honor of a close friend who loves the game more than life, Harry Kalas, I have one last thing to say, something Harry said 548 times:

Outta here, Michael Jack!